N.W.A

Produced by AA Publishing
© AA Media Limited 2013

First published 2003
Second edition 2008
New edition 2013

Published by AA Publishing (a trading name of AA Media Limited, whose registered office is Fanum House, Basing View, Basingstoke, Hampshire RG21 4EA; registered number 06112600)

Researched and written by Beau Riffenburgh and Liz Cruwys
Field checked and updated 2013 by George Keeping, Laurence Mitchell and Clive Tully

Series Management: David Popey
Editor: Ann F Stonehouse
Designer: Tracey Butler
Proofreader: Karen Kemp
Digital imaging & repro: Ian Little
Cartography provided by the Mapping Services Department of AA Publishing

Printed and bound in the UK by Butler, Tanner & Dennis

Mapping in this book is derived from the following products:
OS Landranger 131 (walk 47)
OS Landranger 132 (walks 22, 25, 26, 33–35,37–44)
OS Landranger 133 (walks 8, 9, 13–15, 18–21, 23, 24)
OS Landranger 134 (walks 1– 7, 10, 11)
OS Landranger 143 (walks 45, 48–50)
OS Landranger 144 (walks 17, 30–32, 35)
OS Landranger 156 (walk 12)
OS Explorer 229 (walks 27–29, 36)
OS Explorer 236 (walk 46)
OS Explorer 237 (walk 16)
Contains Ordnance Survey data
© Crown copyright and database right 2013 Ordnance Survey. Licence number 100021153.

A05038

ISBN: 978-0-7495-7484-0
ISBN (SS): 978-0-7495-7510-6

A CIP catalogue record for this book is available from the British Library.

The Automobile Association would like to thank the following photographers, companies and picture libraries for their assistance in the preparation of this book. Abbreviations for the picture credits are as follows: (t) top; (b) bottom; (l) left; (r) right; (AA) AA World Travel Library.

3 AA/T Mackie; 9 AA/A Perkins; 10 AA/T Mackie; 12/13 AA/T Mackie; 20/21 AA/T Mackie; 38/39 AA/T Mackie; 41 AA/T Mackie; 42 AA/R Ireland; 79 AA/T Mackie; 80 AA/T Harris; 100/101 AA/T Mackie; 108/109 AA/T Mackie; 120/121 AA/D Forss; 135 AA/T Mackie; 136 AA/T Mackie

Visit AA Publishing at theAA.com/shop

Right: The beach at Holkham Bay (Walk 33)

50 Walks in
NORFOLK

50 Walks of 2–10 Miles

Contents

The Walks

Following the Walks

An information panel for each walk shows its relative difficulty, the distance and total amount of ascent. An indication of the gradients you will encounter is shown by the rating ▲▲▲ (no steep slopes) to ▲▲▲ (several very steep slopes). Each walk is rated for its relative difficulty compared to the other walks in this book. Walks marked +++ and colour-coded green are likely to be shorter and easier with little total ascent. Those marked with +++ and colour-coded orange are of intermediate difficulty. The hardest walks are marked +++ and colour-coded red.

MAPS

There are 40 maps, covering the 50 walks. Some walks have a suggested option in the same area. The information panel for these walks will tell you how much extra walking is involved. On short-cut suggestions the panel will tell you the total distance if you set out from the start of the main walk. Where an option returns to the same point on the main walk, just the distance of the loop is given. Where an option leaves the main walk at one point and returns to it at another, then the distance shown is for the whole walk. The minimum time suggested is for reasonably fit walkers and doesn't allow for stops. Each walk has a suggested map.

ROUTE MAP LEGEND

──▶──	Walk Route	▭	Built-up Area
❶	Route Waypoint	▭	Woodland Area
─ ─ ─	Adjoining Path	🚻	Toilet
☼	Viewpoint	🅿	Car Park
•	Place of Interest	⊞	Picnic Area
⌂	Steep Section	)(	Bridge

START POINTS

The start of each walk is given as a six-figure grid reference prefixed by two letters indicating which 100km square of the National Grid it refers to. You'll find more information on grid references on most Ordnance Survey, AA Walking and Leisure Maps.

DOGS

We have tried to give dog owners useful advice about how dog friendly each walk is. Please respect other countryside users. Keep your dog under control, especially around livestock, and obey local bylaws and other dog control notices.

CAR PARKING

Many of the car parks suggested are public, but occasionally you may find you have to park on the roadside or in a lay-by. Please be considerate when you leave your car, ensuring that access roads or gates are not blocked and that other vehicles can pass safely.

WALKS LOCATOR

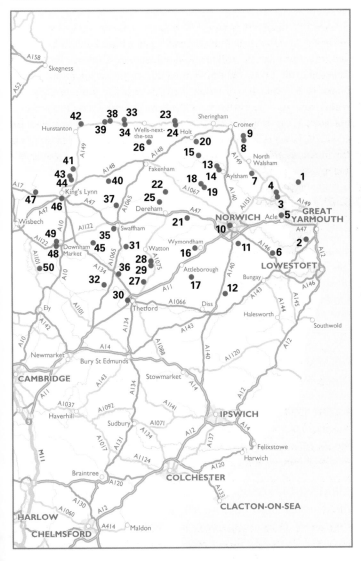

Walking in Norfolk

Reed-fringed lakes, vast sandy beaches, mysterious marshland, teeming wildlife reserves and peaceful, pine-scented forests. Norfolk offers all these and more to walkers, and is one of the most varied and interesting counties in England. It boasts the gorgeous Broads, the wild and heathy Breckland, a stunning coastline and huge areas of fen and marsh. It also has more than its share of long distance footpaths, including the Norfolk Coast and Peddars Way path, the Weavers' Way, Marriott's Way, Hereward Way and Boudicca Way. If you follow the walks in this book you will travel along all these footpaths and a great deal more besides.

AN EXTRAORDINARY LANDSCAPE

Norfolk – and East Anglia in general – has a reputation as being flat and featureless, but the reality could not be more different. The Cromer Ridge and the gently rolling countryside to the south provide some slopes to put your legs through their paces, while you are presented with changing and diverse scenery at every turn. There are medieval fortresses at Castle Rising and Castle Acre, and splendid country houses and stately homes at Blickling, Mannington, Wolferton, Sandringham and Holkham. There are steam railways in the Bure Valley, a dinosaur adventure at Weston Park and bustling market towns with fabulous Georgian architecture. Lonely, ruined priories are reminders of the power the Church once held in this populous county, and there are strongholds raised by the Romans to repel Saxon invasions – see Burgh Castle near Great Yarmouth, Caister St Edmunds near Norwich, and Branodunum at Brancaster. There are pleasure parks on the coast, excellent bird sanctuaries at Welney and Horsey Mere, and farms that fill the air with the sweet scent of lavender, roses and herbs. There are museums, art galleries and theatres. And there are formal gardens, zoos and even the unusual – a 215ft (65m) tall Ecotricity Wind Turbine to climb at Swaffham. In short, Norfolk has it all!

THE WALKS

The book includes a variety of walks, ranging from gentle ambles around nature reserves to longer hikes that take in sections of the long distance trails. Some of the walks are exclusively on footpaths and include routes across farmland and meadows that can be gloriously muddy. Others are along surfaced country lanes that provide easy and level walking. Most offer a combination.

FORAYS INTO NORFOLK

There are four areas within Norfolk that are particularly worth a visit. First, no trip to the county would be complete without a foray into the

Right: Berney Arms Mill, a famous Norfolk landmark on the Yare (Walk 2)

Broads – one of England's best-known National Parks and a region of outstanding beauty. When walking around Horsey, Loddon and Breydon, you will see picturesque lakes with windmills silhouetted on the horizon and boats dotted around the surface. Second, the sandy heaths and coniferous forests of Breckland add to Norfolk's special character, as you will see if you follow the routes around Thetford, Downham Market and Swaffham. Third, few will deny that Norfolk's coast is a fabulous area to walk. There are miles of wide sandy beaches around Hunstanton, where the sea appears as a distant silver line on the horizon, and there are salty marshes full of reeds and grass that wave and hiss in the breeze at Brancaster and Burnham. And, finally, there is west Norfolk, where the Fens merge into marshland, a silent and lonely area where bird calls are the only sound, near Welney and the River Great Ouse.

These walks will allow you to sample the varied delights of all these fabulous areas, and hopefully encourage you to explore this wonderful county further.

PUBLIC TRANSPORT Some of these walks, like the ones beginning in Norwich or Thetford, are easily reached by public transport. Others are remote and rely on cars to get you to the starting point. For information about public transport in the county, call Traveline on 0870 608 2608, or visit www.travelineeastanglia.co.uk. You can obtain mainline railway information from National Train Enquiries on 08457 484950, and you may also find the website www.pti.org.uk a useful source of information.

Above: A track through Thetford Forest (Walk 36)

Walking in Safety

All these walks are suitable for any reasonably fit person, but less experienced walkers should try the easier walks first. Route finding is usually straightforward, but you will find that an Ordnance Survey or AA walking map is a useful addition to the route maps and descriptions; recommendations can be found in the information panels.

RISKS

Although each walk here has been researched with a view to minimising the risks to the walkers who follow its route, no walk in the countryside can be considered to be completely free from risk. Walking in the outdoors will always require a degree of common sense and judgement to ensure that it is as safe as possible.

- Be particularly careful on cliff paths and in upland terrain, where the consequences of a slip can be very serious.
- Remember to check tidal conditions before walking on the seashore.
- Some sections of route are by, or cross, busy roads. Take care and remember traffic is a danger even on minor country lanes.
- Be careful around farmyard machinery and livestock, especially if you have children with you.
- Be aware of the consequences of changes in the weather and check the forecast before you set out. Carry spare clothing and a torch if you are walking in the winter months. Remember the weather can change very quickly at any time of the year, and in moorland and heathland areas, mist and fog can make route finding much harder. Don't set out in these conditions unless you are confident of your navigation skills in poor visibility. In summer remember to take account of the heat and sun; wear a hat and carry water.
- On walks away from centres of population you should carry a whistle and survival bag. If you do have an accident requiring the emergency services, make a note of your position as accurately as possible and dial 999.

COUNTRYSIDE CODE

- Be safe, plan ahead and follow any signs.
- Leave gates and property as you find them.
- Protect plants and animals and take your litter home.
- Keep dogs under close control.
- Consider other people.

For more information visit www.naturalengland.org.uk/ourwork/enjoying/countrysidecode

Overleaf: Sunset on Horsey Mere (Walk 1)

Around Horsey Mere

DISTANCE 3.5 miles (5.7km)   MINIMUM TIME 1hr 30min

ASCENT/GRADIENT Negligible ▲▲▲   LEVEL OF DIFFICULTY ✚✚✚

PATHS Marked trails along dykes (walk quietly to avoid disturbing nesting birds)

LANDSCAPE Reed-fringed drainage channels, marshy lake and water-meadows

SUGGESTED MAP AA Walker's Map 22 The Norfolk Broads

START/FINISH Grid reference: TG456223

DOG FRIENDLINESS On lead on farmland around livestock; avoid areas used by nesting water birds

PARKING National Trust pay-and-display at Horsey Drainage Mill

PUBLIC TOILETS At car park

In 1938 a devastating combination of high tides and storms occurred around Horsey. The sea surged inland, flooding buildings and fields, and forcing people to evacuate their homes. It was four months before the water subsided and the villagers were able to resume normal life, although it took another five years before the damaging effects of salt water on the fields was finally overcome and crops could be grown again. Horsey is barely 3ft (1m) above sea level and, as you walk around the reed-fringed mere and stroll along its many drainage channels, you will appreciate the unchanging wildness of this part of Norfolk and its vulnerability at the hands of the sea. Not for nothing was this area known as 'Devil's Country' in local legends.

LISTING BROGRAVE MILL

You will see part of the Devil's handiwork when you pass Brograve Mill, between Horsey and Waxham. The story goes that one Thomas Brograve was determined to reclaim part of this wilderness for farming, and built a mill. The Devil was furious and tried to blow it down. He did not succeed, but you will see a distinct list to the mill today, indicating that the battle was a close-run thing!

The village and surrounding area is now in the care of the National Trust, so its picturesque tranquillity is unlikely to be spoiled. All Saints' Church dates from the 13th century and has an attractive thatched nave. Go inside and look for the stained-glass window in the south chancel commemorating Catherine Ursula Rising, who died in 1890. She is shown painting in her drawing room at nearby Horsey Hall.

HORSEY DRAINAGE MILL

The village's most famous feature is the Horsey Drainage Mill, built to pump water from the surrounding farmland. It dates from the middle of the 19th century, but was rebuilt in 1897 and again in 1912. It has four storeys of brick, and a handsome weather-boarded cap in the shape of a boat. It was working in 1940 when it was struck by lightning, and was restored in 1961. Today it is owned by the National Trust and is open to visitors.

To the southwest is Horsey Mere, a part of the Broads and a beautiful stretch of the walk. The mere is surrounded by reed beds, which provide the raw materials for thatching many of Horsey's pretty houses. This peaceful stretch of water offers a haven for countless birds, particularly in winter.

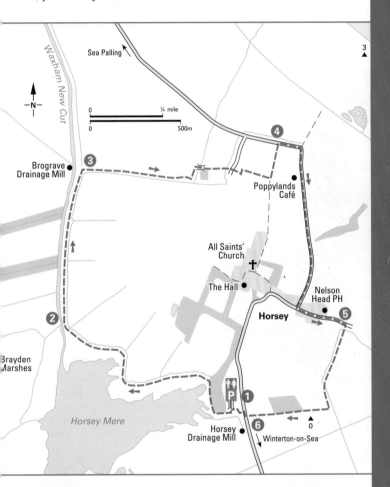

1 From the National Trust car park walk towards the toilets and take the footpath to the right of them. This leads to a footbridge. After crossing the bridge turn immediately right and follow the path along the

side of Horsey Mere through reeds and alder copses.

2 Turn right when the path meets a brown-watered dyke (Waxham New Cut). Eventually you will see derelict Brograve Drainage Mill ahead. Herons and other birds often perch on its battered sails, so it's worth stopping to look.

3 Turn right immediately adjacent to the mill and walk along the edge of a field. Reed beds give way to water-meadow. Continue straight ahead. The path bends left, then right across a footbridge, then crosses a small lane and continues through the field opposite. At the end of the field, make a sharp left, eventually coming to another lane.

4 Go right at the lane, bearing right where it meets a track, and walk past Poppylands Café. When you reach a junction turn left, following the sign for the Nelson Head. Pass the pub on your left-hand side, then look for a well-defined footpath going off to your right.

5 Walk past the gate and continue along the wide sward ahead, with a narrow dyke on either side. When the sward divides, bear left and head for a stile at the end of the footpath. Climb this and immediately turn right to walk along a spacious field. This area is used for grazing breeding stock and you should look for signs warning about the presence of bulls. Since this part of the walk is permissive, and not a public footpath, the National Trust is within its rights to put bulls here, so it is important to check for warning signs before you venture forth. These are always prominently displayed. If this is the case, you will have to walk back to the lane and turn left. This will take you back to the car park at the start of the walk.

6 Assuming there are no bulls to hinder your progress, climb the stile, between the field and the road, and then cross the road. The car park where the walk began is ahead of you and slightly to your right. This is a good time to explore the delights of restored Horsey Drainage Mill, which you will find just to your left.

WHERE TO EAT AND DRINK The Nelson Head, owned by the National Trust, serves food and fine ales (opening times vary throughout the year). You can also try the Poppylands Café at Delph Farm along the way, which offers snacks and breakfasts. Staithe Stores at the car park sells snacks that can be eaten on the grass around the pleasant car park and wharfs.

WHAT TO SEE Horsey Mere attracts hundreds of wigeon in winter, along with teal, shoveller, pochard, gadwall, goldeneye and tufted duck. Bitterns may be seen at any time of year. Look for stonechats, yellow wagtails and grasshopper warblers if you head towards the dunes. You might also spot two rare warblers – Cetti's and Savi's. The former is a newcomer, and the latter is returning to areas where it was once common.

WHILE YOU'RE THERE Nearby Hickling Broad is an unspoiled bird reserve in the care of Norfolk Wildlife Trust. It is home to Britain's largest butterfly – the swallowtail. To the south, Rollesby Broad is linked to the Ormesby and Filby broads. To the south of Horsey is the Winterton Dunes National Nature Reserve, some 269 acres (109ha) of sand and marsh that is a fine place to watch migrant birds of prey and other species.

Breydon Water and Burgh Castle

DISTANCE 8 miles (12.9km)   MINIMUM TIME 3hrs

ASCENT/GRADIENT 49ft (15m) ▲▲▲   LEVEL OF DIFFICULTY +++

PATHS Riverside paths, footpaths, busy stretch of road, several steps

LANDSCAPE Marshland, expanses of mudflats and some arable land

SUGGESTED MAP AA Walker's Map 22 The Norfolk Broads

START/FINISH Grid reference: TG476050

DOG FRIENDLINESS Must be on lead at all times along edge of Breydon Water

PARKING Car park near Church Farm Hotel

PUBLIC TOILETS None on route

Near the western reaches of Breydon Water there is a Roman fort, a wind pump owned by the National Trust and an atmospheric pub, which is inaccessible to cars. However, there is an obstacle preventing you from wandering to and from these sites: the River Yare. At the start of the walk you will see the river begin to widen, until it forms the vast, silt-slippery flats of Breydon Water that lies between the Roman castle and the mill and pub – so the only way to see all three on foot is to walk around it.

This part of the Broads is perhaps the most mysterious and lonely of all, and the fact that few roads cross the marshes that radiate out from Breydon Water means that it is generally people-free. This suits birds very nicely, and the Royal Society for the Protection of Birds (RSPB) manages quite a large part of it. Halvergate Marshes, to the west, is an alluvial basin that is home to shovellers, snipe, lapwings, yellow wagtails and redshanks.

Berney Arms Mill is one of the most spectacular mills in the country. It is in perfect working order and stands some 70ft (21m) high, making it the tallest marsh mill in Norfolk or Suffolk. It was built in 1870 and now houses a small museum. Downstream is the Berney Arms pub, accessible only to people who walk or navigate the silty channels in their boats.

AN IMPRESSIVE FORTRESS

Gariannonum, or Burgh Castle, lies on the opposite shore of the river. Originally this would have commanded an imposing position looking towards Caister, but changes in the sea level and silting up have relegated it to a quiet part of the river. It was built in the 3rd century AD to defend the Roman province from marauding Saxons, and was an impressive fortress. Even today, visitors will see walls rising to more than 15ft (5m). This stronghold is said to have been the place where the Irish missionary St Fursey arrived in England in about AD 630. One of the first things he did was to found a monastery, which he called Cnobheresburg, although nothing remains of this today. The saint himself moved later to France; after his death his body parts were split up, and his head is still revered in Péronne, Picardy.

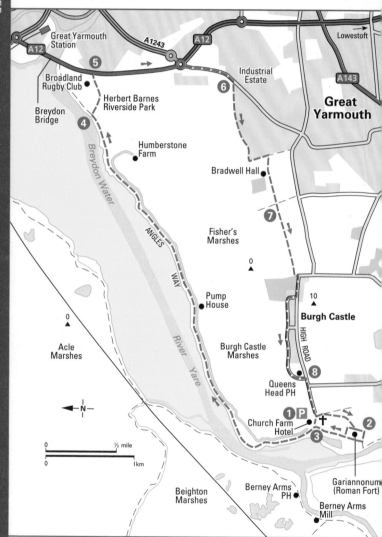

1 Leave the car park and walk uphill towards the church. Take the path to the left of the church, through a kissing gate, signposted to the castle. After a few steps and another kissing gate, you will see a well-trodden path cutting diagonally across the fields. Follow this until you reach the spectacularly grand walls of the Roman fort Gariannonum, aiming for the gap in the middle.

2 Go through the gap to explore the castle, then head for 28 steps in the far right-hand corner. Descend the steps, walk alongside a field, and look for 40 steps leading down to the river bank. Turn right along the Angles Way and continue until you reach a junction of paths behind Church Farm Hotel. This stretch of riverside and reedbeds may be flooded after heavy rain.

3 Turn left towards the double gates, which will take you on a long uninterrupted trail (3 miles/4.8km) along the edge of Breydon Water. The path sticks closely by the river, following a raised flood bank, with glorious views in all directions across the pancake-flat marshes and mudflats. Eventually, you will see the tall struts of Breydon Bridge in the distance.

4 Pass through a gate to enter the Herbert Barnes Riverside Park. When the path divides, take the right-hand fork, leaving the river and winding across a meadow to Broadland Rugby Club, where you climb to the A12.

5 If you want to avoid a busy stretch of main road, turn around at this point and retrace your steps along the river, enjoying the views of Breydon Water in the opposite direction. Otherwise, turn right on the A12,

keeping carefully to the right-hand verge, and continue for just over 0.5 miles (800m) to a roundabout with Gapton Hall Retail Park on your right. Keep right on a pedestrian and cycle path beside the road. After passing the entrance signs for Bradwell and just before an industrial estate, look for a gap in the hedge and steps leading down to a bridleway across the marshes on your right.

6 Turn down the footpath, which takes you between the estate and the marshes. After 0.75 miles (1.2km), turn left onto a wide track for about 250yds (229m), then take a footpath through a gap in the hedge to your right, past the farm buildings of Bradwell Hall, to a crossroads.

7 Keep ahead through a rusty gate and pass to the left of an abandoned house, then follow the path between the fields. Cross a stile and go across the field to another stile and a short farm track, which bends left to arrive at High Road. Turn right, and right again onto Back Lane. This quiet lane bends left, passing houses and an Anglian Water station, before emerging onto High Road at the Queens Head.

8 Turn right and keep climbing until you see the church. Turn right into the car park.

WHERE TO EAT AND DRINK Church Farm Hotel serves food at lunchtime and evenings, with hog roasts on summer Sundays. There is a garden, with a children's play area. The Queens Head at Burgh Castle also serves home-cooked food, and has a garden and play area.

WHAT TO SEE More rare birds were once shot on Breydon Water than anywhere else in Britain, but it is now a nature reserve covering some 1,100 acres (445ha).

WHILE YOU'RE THERE Great Yarmouth to the east has the Pleasure Beach, with rides and attractions. Pleasurewood Hills, between Great Yarmouth and Lowestoft, is a huge theme park with roller coasters, water rides and other attractions.

Overleaf: Boats at rest on Hickling Broad (Walk 4)

Ludham and the Broads

DISTANCE 5 miles (8km)	MINIMUM TIME 2hrs

ASCENT/GRADIENT 33ft (10m) ▲▲▲   LEVEL OF DIFFICULTY ✦✦✦

PATHS Quiet country lanes and grassy footpaths

LANDSCAPE Reed-fringed broad and gently rolling agricultural land

SUGGESTED MAP AA Walker's Map 22 The Norfolk Broads

START/FINISH Grid reference: TG391180

DOG FRIENDLINESS Not permitted in nature reserve; on lead through farmland

PARKING Womack Staithe in Horsefen Road, Ludham

PUBLIC TOILETS At Womack Staithe

No visit to Norfolk would be complete without a trip to the Broads National Park. This is a patchwork of interlinked streams, lakes and channels that wind sluggishly over the flat land to the east of Norwich. Three major rivers – the Bure, Waveney and Yare – supply most of the water to the meres, ponds and marshes before entering the great tidal basin at Breydon Water and flowing into the sea at Great Yarmouth.

Despite the fact that the Broads comprise one of England's best wilderness areas, most natural historians and archaeologists accept that their origin lies in ancient human activity. They were formed when local people mined the extensive peat deposits here, cutting away the fuel to form neat vertical sides. So how did these ancient folk, with their primitive tools, carve out these huge areas before they filled up? The answer lies in the fact that the sea level was lower in the past and none of the Broads is very deep, mostly less than 15ft (4.5m), suggesting the peat was cut until it became too boggy.

So, when did all this happen? No one really knows, since maps of the area are lacking until about 400 years ago. Fritton and the linked Ormesby–Rollesby–Filby broads appear on a map of 1574, and Domesday records indicate that there was demand for peat from Norwich and Great Yarmouth. Documents written in the 13th and 14th centuries tell of devastating floods, and mention that turf production around South Walsham declined dramatically. Perhaps it was then that the miners abandoned their workings and left the area to become a paradise for native birds and plants.

New industries sprang up, using sedge and reed for thatching and alder wood for brush making. These small-scale projects kept the waterways open. Their decline has meant that open fenland has gradually become dense alder carr (woodland). Ancient waterways that once saw traditional craft transporting goods are silting up, and the heavy use of fertilisers on arable land causes algal blooms. To see what the Broads Authority is doing about it, visit How Hill nature reserve.

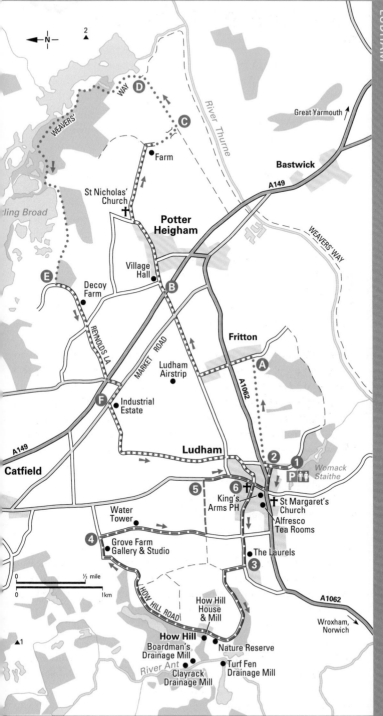

① Leave the car park and the busy marina and walk up Horsefen Road, going the same way that you came in to park.

② Turn left at the end of Horsefen Road, walking along the footpath that runs inside a hedge next to the road. When you see the King's Arms ahead, turn right up the road towards 'Catfield'. After a few paces turn left onto School Road. Houses soon give way to countryside. Take the permissive path on the right of a hedge next to the road. Go straight across the next junction, following the sign for How Hill.

③ Turn right along a lane signposted 'How Hill'. The lane winds and twists, and is fairly narrow, which makes for pleasant walking. You will soon reach How Hill House, a sail-less windmill and How Hill nature reserve. There are marked trails through the reserve, if you feel like a pleasant diversion. When you have finished, continue down How Hill Road. Pass Grove Farm Gallery and Studio on your right, and

look for a red-brick barn, followed by a lane, also on your right.

④ Turn right down Wateringpiece Lane. Pass the modern water tower on your left and walk past some fields. Look for the public footpath crossing the road. Go left along the bridleway that runs along the edge of a field until it ends at a lane.

⑤ Turn right on Catfield Road and walk along the verge on the right, where there is a footpath. This road can be busy in the summer, when thousands of visitors flock to Ludham and How Hill. Ignore the lane on your left, heading to Potter Heigham, and continue walking ahead until you reach a crossroads by Ludham Methodist Church.

⑥ Go straight across, walking a few paces until you reach the next junction with Ludham Church ahead of you. Turn left along Yarmouth Road, then right into Horsefen Road. This will take you back to the car park.

WHERE TO EAT AND DRINK At Ludham the friendly King's Arms has a pleasant beer garden with a playground for children, and serves good food and real ale. Just around the corner are the Alfresco Tea Rooms.

WHAT TO SEE At How Hill you can visit Toad Hole, a marshman's cottage built in the 18th century, now furnished to look like a fen labourer's home. The best drainage mills are also near How Hill. Turf Fen (1880s) is on the opposite bank of the River Ant, and Boardman's Mill (similar date with a 1926 engine) is to the north. Further north is Clayrack Mill, restored in 1988.

WHILE YOU'RE THERE Fairhaven Woodland and Water Garden is located on South Walsham Inner Broad and offers visitors superb gardens and boat trips. You'll find hire boats and trips at Wroxham and Potter Heigham. The Broadland Conservation Centre at Ranworth provides information and maps, and is a good place to start any serious exploration of the surrounding area.

Hickling Broad

DISTANCE 8.75 miles (14.1km)   MINIMUM TIME 3hrs 30min

ASCENT/GRADIENT 49ft (15m) ▲▲▲   LEVEL OF DIFFICULTY +++

SEE MAP AND INFORMATION PANEL FOR WALK 3

Drainage mills still play an important role in the Broads, and there are plenty to see around Ludham. They stand alone and proud in this flat landscape, so that a tower silhouetted against a sunset or reflected in still waters is an image that many visitors take home with them. Mills are as much a part of the landscape here as the many birds that come to feed or breed.

Mills come in many different shapes and sizes. Tower windmills use wind power to drive their scooping mechanisms. Others, including some designed by the famous millwright Dan England, were fitted with powerful turbine engines in the 20th century. Hollow-post mills were used in the 17th century – the sail mechanism and cap sit atop a hollow post. These were found to be temperamental and later fell into disuse. The one at How Hill (Clayrack Drainage Mill) was discovered at nearby Ranworth, and rebuilt in 1988.

Go right at the end of Horsefen Road at Point ❷, and look for the bridleway on your right. This runs through fields to a lane at Point ❹. Turn left, cross the A1062 and, at the next T-junction, turn right and continue across Market Road to the A149. Cross this, through the red and white barriers, heading for School Road opposite, Point ❸.

Walk into Potter Heigham, going straight on at the next junction, with the Victorian school and village hall on your left. This becomes Church Road, and you pass St Nicholas' Church on your left. Go right down Marsh Road until you reach a farm. Bear right on the track before crossing a footbridge with Broads Authority footpath markers, and bear left at a T-junction, Point ❸.

At the next junction you reach the Weavers' Way, Point ❹, where you turn left. This winds through reed beds along the edge of Hickling Broad. Go through a gate, then continue along the way. The reserve ends at another gate at Point ❺. Turn left on the lane, past Decoy Farm, then go straight across at the next crossroads to Reynolds Lane.

Cross the A149, walk a few paces, then turn right. Go left after the industrial estate at Point ❻, and follow this lane when it makes a sharp left. Walk for about 0.75 miles (1.2km), going straight at the first junction and right at the second, until you reach Point ❻.

Acle and the Bure Valley

DISTANCE 4.75 miles (7.7km)   MINIMUM TIME 2hrs

ASCENT/GRADIENT 49ft (15m) ▲▲▲   LEVEL OF DIFFICULTY ✛✛✛

PATHS Mostly narrow paths along river banks and across fields

LANDSCAPE Windmill-studded marshes and rural marshland

SUGGESTED MAP AA Walker's Map 22 The Norfolk Broads

START/FINISH Grid reference: TG401107

DOG FRIENDLINESS Dogs should be on lead on agricultural land

PARKING Free car park off Bridewell Lane, near library

PUBLIC TOILETS None on route

The name Acle comes from an old Saxon word meaning oak grove, and this ancient settlement is recorded in the Domesday Book of 1086 as having 23 villagers, 38 smallholders, 3 slaves and 40 pigs. Later, as the town continued to thrive, its occupants needed to travel further afield to sell their wares and buy other commodities, so a bridge was built in 1101 and named Weybrigg. An Augustinian cell was founded close by in 1225, and took its name from the bridge to become Weybrigg Priory. The priory fell victim to the Dissolution in 1536, and the stone from its walls was taken by locals.

Acle continued to prosper in the 13th century, when it was granted a charter to hold a market, and in Tudor times hundreds of oaks were felled to provide timber to build Elizabeth I's navy. In the 19th century Acle developed a lucrative boatbuilding trade, and boatyards sprang up all along the River Bure between Acle Bridge and Boat Dyke. It must have been a spectacular sight in 1890 when Acle's first regatta was held and 150 yachts took to the water.

In 1883 the Great Eastern Railway opened a link between Acle and Great Yarmouth, and later the line was extended to Brundall to connect with the existing Norwich–Great Yarmouth line. When the Acle straight opened in 1831, it knocked 3.5 miles (5.7 kms) off the road journey from Acle to Great Yarmouth, cutting out the rather more circuitous route via Fleggburgh. There has been pressure in modern times to widen the road or make it a dual carriageway in order to improve traffic flow, but the stumbling block has been that the Acle straight passes through one of the most sensitive areas of the Broads.

While the town itself has seen development and expansion, it still has a traditional character at its heart, with people flocking here on Thursdays for the market. Equidistant from Norwich and Great Yarmouth, today Acle is known as the 'Gateway to the Broads', which holds true whether you happen to be a pleasure boater, tourist, angling enthusiast, cyclist or walker.

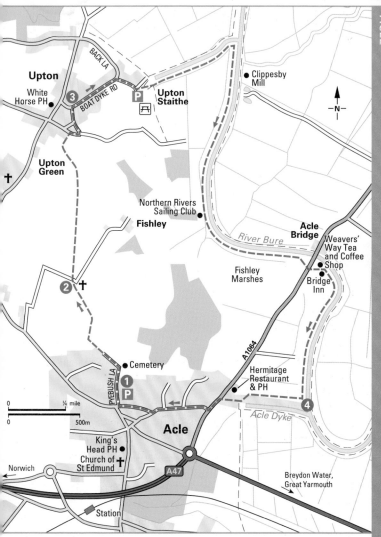

1 Leave the car park, turn right onto Bridewell Lane, and look for Pyebush Lane on your right. Walk down this, passing the recreation ground on your right, to the cemetery at the end. Turn left where the gravel track soon becomes a narrow path through fields. It is well signposted, but the isolated little church at Fishley is a useful landmark.

2 When you draw level with the church, continue along the footpath

and walk through a vast field, then a smaller one. The path then becomes enclosed by hedges and trees. It jigs right and emerges onto a lane next to a large pink house. Turn right, then go left when you reach The Green.

3 Go right, along Boat Dyke Road, and keep right at the junction with Back Lane. When you see a 'No Through Road' sign, go left into the car park and head for Upton Staithe. Bear right and aim for the path along

the right-hand side of the water. Go straight ahead, along the staithe that eventually reaches the River Bure. You can see at least five drainage mills from here: Palmer's, Tall Mill, Oby, Clippesby and Fleggburgh. At the end of Upton Dyke the path swings right along the river. This is a great place for boat-watching, which can be restful or amusing, depending on the experience and skill of the captains. Pass the Northern Rivers Sailing Club, keeping straight on along the river bank. Continue until you see Acle Bridge (once graced with an arch dating from 1830, but this was replaced by steel in 1931). When you reach the boatyard, follow the path to the right, then the left and cross the A1064 carefully. (If the road is very busy, use the crossing point at the brow of the bridge, where you have maximum visibility in both directions.) Aim for the Bridge Inn, which was once part of Weybrigg Priory, founded by Henry III. Make your way through

the pub gardens, looking for the public footpath markers near the sign 'No Glasses Beyond this Point'. This is the Weavers' Way, and you walk along a raised grassy bank for a few steps before it becomes lined by tall reeds. It jigs inland for a short distance, but then rejoins the river until you reach Acle Dyke. At this point, the path is forced right.

4 Walk along the path, past boats bobbing at their moorings, until you reach a tiny gate. Go through this, cross a track and go through a second gate. This leads to a lane. The Weavers' Way heads away to the left, but you continue straight ahead until you reach the Hermitage Restaurant and Public House. Cross the road ahead, bear left, then immediately right and walk along the pavement, passing The Drive. At the junction bear right onto Bridewell Road, following the signs for the car park, which is on your right.

WHERE TO EAT AND DRINK Acle offers a variety of places to eat and drink, including the King's Head in the town centre. At Upton there is the charming White Horse. The Bridge Inn, where the A1064 crosses the River Bure, serves good food, as does the Weavers' Way tea and coffee shop at the same location. The Hermitage Restaurant and Public House has delightful riverbank gardens.

WHAT TO SEE The Church of St Edmund has a 13th-century tower and a Norman doorway. Its most unusual features are two porches, both with upper and lower floors. Portrayed on the north porch are two people praying. One is possibly Robert Bataly, who left 20 marks (a little over £6) for a new porch in 1497.

WHILE YOU'RE THERE Acle is a good place to begin visits to Halvergate Marshes and Breydon Water. Thrigby Hall Wildlife Gardens to the northeast has tigers and crocodiles, as well as a collection of birds. In nearby Tunstall the village pond is said to lead directly to hell...

Around Hardley Flood from Chedgrave

DISTANCE 5.25 miles (8.4km)   MINIMUM TIME 2hrs 15min

ASCENT/GRADIENT 98ft (30m) ▲▲▲   LEVEL OF DIFFICULTY ✚✚✚

PATHS Footpaths along waterways, farm tracks, paved roads

LANDSCAPE Reed-fringed riverside and lakeside, farmland

SUGGESTED MAP AA Walker's Map 22 The Norfolk Broads

START/FINISH Grid reference: TM363987

DOG FRIENDLINESS On lead, especially around Hardley Flood nature reserve

PARKING Car park (pay-and-display) on Church Plain in Loddon (opposite Holy Trinity Church); or Loddon Staithe car park (pay-and-display) near river

PUBLIC TOILETS At both car parks

If you are interested in hidden gems of architecture then Loddon is the place for you, with buildings ranging from a medieval church to some of the largest council houses built to house the London overspill after World War II.

Handsome Holy Trinity Church, on Church Plain, dates from the end of the 15th century – the height of Gothic Perpendicular – and is beautifully light and airy. Its showpiece is the two-storey porch with a spiral staircase and gorgeous carvings. The library, dating from the mid-19th century, was originally a school and was converted to its present use in the 1970s.

Attractive 17th- and 18th-century houses line the High Street, including one curiously called The Institute. Loddon House is perhaps the most ambitious building. It dates from 1711 and has five bays and a glorious collection of columns. It is not to be confused with Loddon Hall, which is located a mile (1.6km) southeast of the village.

CHARMING COUNCIL HOMES

When Loddon became one of the many towns designated for new housing estates to help solve the post-war accommodation crisis, the Lowestoft architects Herbert Taylor and David Green were commissioned to design single-storey retirement homes. Those built in Davy Place are charming, and the 78 homes in Hobart Road, Crossway Terrace and Drury Lane are spacious and of interest, demonstrating that council guidelines and limited finances need not always produce dull results.

Loddon is famous for its watermill. This glorious building spans the River Chet and comprises a weather-boarded mill – dating mostly from the 18th century, although parts are older – with an early 19th-century house attached to it. It is not open to the public.

This walk takes you through some of Norfolk's most attractive countryside, giving a taste of the silent and mysterious Broads and peaceful farmland, as well as sampling the delights of watching the different boats as they jostle and jangle on their moorings along the banks of the busy River Chet.

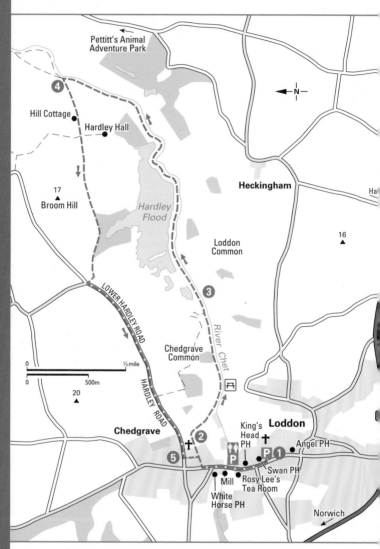

❶ Turn right past the library onto Bridge Street and walk down the hill to cross the river into Chedgrave. At the White Horse go right, then look for the public footpath on your right immediately after the row of terraced houses, where there is a short length of railing along the kerb. Meet a residential street, cross it to the footpath which runs between hedges opposite, and continue to Chedgrave Church. Follow the footpath until you meet a lane.

2 Turn right, passing a meadow on your left before going through a small gate at the public footpath sign. Continue on the path along the north bank of the River Chet.

3 Continue along the river path. Depending on the growth of reeds, you may be able to see that you are on a causeway here, with the Chet on your right and the meres that comprise Hardley Flood on your left. It is well worth pausing here if you are interested in birding, as the Norfolk Wildlife Trust has erected nesting areas in the water, and there is a public hide on the footpath from which you can observe the abundant birdlife. Continue along this path until broad gives way to farmland and you can see Hardley Hall off to your left. The path then goes through a final gate to meet a wide farm track.

4 Turn left on the farm track. Go up a hill, passing Hill Cottage on your right-hand side, then Hardley Hall on your left. The farm track ends here at a lane. Continue straight ahead on a bridleway towards some woodland. Walk along this lane until you reach Lower Hardley Road and a sign pointing left to Loddon. (Don't be tempted to take the left-hand footpath further down the road, which heads to Chedgrave Common.) Ignore Pits Lane on the left, signed 'No Through Road', and continue walking to the gravelled drive on the left.

5 Take this turning, signposted to the church. When you reach the church, look for the grassy footpath to the right which leads back towards the road. Retrace your steps along the footpath, go left on the main road, across the river and walk up the hill to the car park.

WHERE TO EAT AND DRINK Both the Angel and the Swan in Loddon serve good food, as does the White Horse over the river in Chedgrave. Loddon's King's Head (morning coffee, lunches and evening meals) is near the police station, and Rosy Lee's Tea Room is near the bridge. Loddon also offers a variety of takeaways, plus several general stores should you fancy a picnic (there is a picnic site at Loddon Staithe, and beside the Chet at Pye's Mill).

WHAT TO SEE There is only one all-timber mill in England, at Loddon on the River Chet. Meanwhile, a corner of the graveyard of Holy Trinity Church is unusual in that it has been set aside as a nature reserve. The church itself dates from the end of the 15th century and is very light and airy inside. Don't miss the superb painting of Sir James Hobart and his wife.

WHILE YOU'RE THERE Hales Hall was built by Sir James Hobart in the 1470s (Hobart in Australia was named after his family). He was Attorney General to Henry VII and wealthy enough to build himself a substantial mansion. It houses Reads Nursery and the national collection of citrus fruits. Pettitt's Animal Adventure Park is to the northeast, and nearby Raveningham Gardens are well signposted from the village centre.

A Loop to the East of Worstead

DISTANCE 4 miles (6.4km)	MINIMUM TIME 1hr 45min

ASCENT/GRADIENT 33ft (10m) ▲▲▲   LEVEL OF DIFFICULTY ✚✚✚

PATHS Easy public footpaths and some paved country lanes

LANDSCAPE Woodland and agricultural land

SUGGESTED MAP AA Walker's Map 22 The Norfolk Broads

START/FINISH Grid reference: TG302260

DOG FRIENDLINESS Dogs should be under strict control on lanes

PARKING On Church Plain

PUBLIC TOILETS In pub car park (follow signposts)

Edward III was blessed with a faithful and loyal wife, who bore him 12 children and exerted a moderating influence on his fiery Plantagenet temper. Her name was Philippa of Hainault, and she was the daughter of William, Count of Hainault and Zeeland. Her Flemish background made her something of an expert on the weaving trade, and it was because of Philippa that so many experienced weavers settled in Norfolk and Suffolk.

As far as medieval marriages went, Edward and Philippa's was made in heaven. He was not faithful and she was not beautiful, but they maintained a close attachment throughout their long liaison. Their children included the Black Prince, who died just two years before his long-lived father without ever taking the throne; and the intelligent, powerful John of Gaunt, who was easily one of the richest men in the world in his lifetime. All the King's children remained on surprisingly good terms with each other and their father, something largely attributed to Philippa's gentle nature.

FLEMISH WEAVERS

As soon as she had settled in England, Philippa realised that it did not make economic sense for vast quantities of fine wool to be produced in East Anglia for export to Flanders, where weavers made it into cloth and sold it back to the English at inflated prices. She encouraged Flemish weavers to settle in England, so they could train Englishmen in cloth production. Worstead was one of several villages that profited from their expertise. The so-called 'Worstead villages' included North Walsham, Scottow, Tunstead and Aylsham, but it was Worstead that gave its name to the light, relatively inexpensive cloth that made these places so rich.

By the end of the 14th century it was not the weavers of Ypres and Ghent who were setting world standards in cloth excellence, but those of Norfolk and Suffolk. John Paston wrote in 1465 that 'I would make my doublet all worsted, for worship of Norfolk.'

In 1379 the weavers' guild was so wealthy and powerful that its members pooled their resources and built St Mary's Church, declaring that the original St Andrew's Church was neither large nor grand enough for their village. The result is one of the loveliest parish churches in the county, with a tower that is 109ft (33m) tall, and the church itself 130ft (40m) long – astonishing proportions for a village church.

Weaving in Worstead continued until the late 19th century and is practised on a much smaller scale today by some local people.

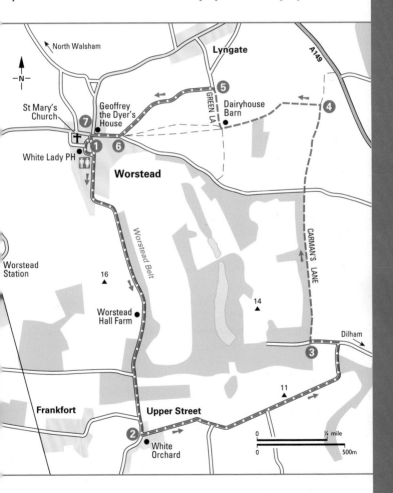

❶ From Church Plain, in the centre of Worstead, turn right onto Front Street, with handsome 14th-century St Mary's Church behind you and the

White Lady pub on your right. Bend to the left, then immediately right and continue walking out of the village. The road veers to the left, then to the right. The mixed deciduous plantation to your left is called the Worstead Belt because of its long, thin shape. Pass Worstead Hall Farm (originally 16th century) on your right before plunging into shady woodland.

2 Turn left on the road signposted to Dilham. Ignore the two lanes off to the right, but follow the road round to the left when it bends sharply through woods and up a hill. Where the road turns sharp right, turn left onto the concrete lane and continue ahead until you reach a sign, stating 'Private Road'.

3 Turn right and walk along the wide track (marked as a public footpath) that leads in a straight line through a tunnel of mixed woodland. This is Carman's Lane, and it emerges onto a quiet country lane after about 0.5 miles (800m). Cross the lane, heading for the footpath opposite. There is a hedge right in front of you, with fields on either side, and a footpath sign. Keep to the left of the hedge and walk along the edge of the field until you see the sign for another footpath off to your left.

4 Turn left along this path, walking until the red roofs of Dairyhouse Barn come into view. Just after this, there is a T-junction of footpaths. Take the one to the right, a farm track called Green Lane, and walk along it until you reach a paved road.

5 Go left along a lane that is bordered by tall hedgerows – these are filled with nesting birds in the spring. You pass a few neat houses on your left before the lane ends in a T-junction.

6 Turn right opposite Rose Cottage and Windy Ridge onto Honing Row, and walk for a few paces until you reach Geoffrey the Dyer's House on your right. This dates from the 16th century, and has unusually tall ceilings in order to accommodate the merchant's looms. The site of the old manor house lies up this lane, too.

7 Turn left opposite Geoffrey's house to return to your parking place and the start of the walk.

WHERE TO EAT AND DRINK The pleasant and friendly White Lady pub in Worstead offers real ale, occasional hog roasts and excellent burgers and chips. Children are welcome, and there is some outdoor seating for warm summer days. In winter the pub is filled with the scent of wood fires.

WHAT TO SEE Worstead House, built by James Wyatt between 1791 and 1797 for Sir George Berney Brograve, was a grand affair with three bays and a big central bow. By the 20th century it had become a little shabby, and in the 1930s it was bought by Harold Harmsworth, Viscount Rothermere, the newspaper mogul. He demolished the hall, intending to rebuild it, but World War II changed his plans, and Worstead remains without its hall.

WHILE YOU'RE THERE Nearby North Walsham (about 3 miles/4.8km to the north) was a centre for the wool trade in the 14th century, producing 'Walsham cloth' that was lighter than worsted. This allowed the villagers to build handsome St Nicholas' Church near the Market Cross. Horatio Nelson attended the Paston School here. A battle took place close by on 22 June, 1381, marking a bloody end to Norfolk's part in the Peasants' Revolt.

Overstrand to Northrepps

DISTANCE 4 miles (6.4km)	MINIMUM TIME 2hrs

ASCENT/GRADIENT 295ft (90m) ▲▲▲ LEVEL OF DIFFICULTY +++

PATHS Farm tracks, footpaths, quiet lanes

LANDSCAPE Attractive rolling farmland

SUGGESTED MAP OS Explorer 252 Norfolk Coast East

START/FINISH Grid reference: TG247410

DOG FRIENDLINESS Dogs not allowed on Promenade

PARKING Pay-and-display car park on Coast Road in Overstrand

PUBLIC TOILETS At car park

There is a constant battle raging between the sea and the land at Overstrand, and although the land is holding its own thanks to some serious sea defences, it looks as though the water will be the eventual winner. The cliffs around Overstrand are crumbling slowly and are being reclaimed by the North Sea. Further east, the cliffs are so precarious that there is no access to them until you reach Mundesley. In the 14th century the sea swept away the land on which St Martin's Church stood, and the villagers were obliged to build another – the one you can see today.

This walk wanders through Poppylands, the name given to the area by poet Clement William Scott in late Victorian times. Scott loved this part of Norfolk and wrote a series of newspaper articles about the unspoiled beauty of its fishing villages, rolling farmland and rugged coastline. His descriptions were so vivid that visitors flocked to the area, and the humble fishing village developed to accommodate the rich and famous. Houses were designed by prominent architects like Edwin Lutyens and Arthur William Bloomfield. The Pleasaunce was designed by Lutyens with gardens by Gertrude Jekyll for Gladstone's Chief Whip, Lord Battersea, and splendid Overstrand Hall was built for the banker Lord Hillingdon in 1899. Even the Churchill family had a residence here.

As the population grew to include an upper-class community, more facilities were needed to accommodate them. St Martin's Church had become unsafe in the 18th century, and Christ Church was raised in 1867 to replace it. But the newcomers preferred the ancient simplicity of St Martin's and so it was rebuilt and restored between 1911and 1914. There was also a handsome Methodist chapel, designed in 1898 by Lutyens, with a brick lower floor, and arched clerestory windows above.

After strolling through the farmland south of Overstrand you reach Northrepps, which became famous when Verily Anderson wrote a book, *The Northrepps Grandchildren*, describing life at Northrepps Hall.

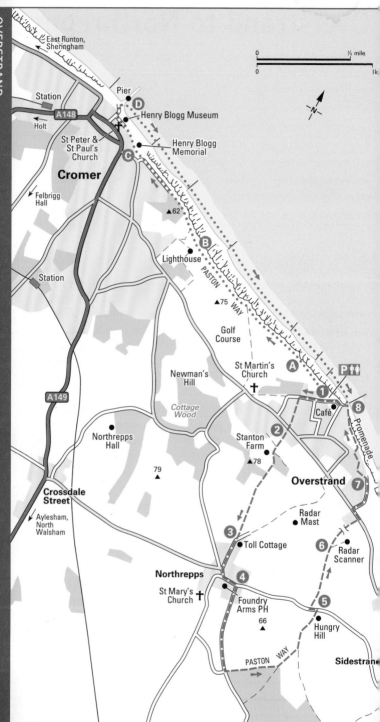

East Runton, Sheringham

Pier

Station

A148

Holt

D Henry Blogg Museum

St Peter & St Paul's Church

Henry Blogg Memorial

C

Cromer

Felbrigg Hall

Station

▲62

B Lighthouse

PASTON WAY

▲75

Golf Course

St Martin's Church

A

P

Newman's Hill

1

Café

Cottage Wood

8

A149

2

Northrepps Hall

Stanton Farm

▲78

Overstrand

79 ▲

Radar Mast

7

Crossdale Street

Aylesham, North Walsham

3 Toll Cottage

6 Radar Scanner

Northrepps

4

St Mary's Church

Foundry Arms PH

5 Hungry Hill

66 ▲

PASTON WAY

Sidestran

½ mile

0   1k

1 Go right, out of the car park onto Paul's Lane. Pass the Old Rectory, then walk along the pavement on the left. Pass Arden Close, then look for the public footpath sign on your left. Follow this alley until you reach a road.

2 Cross the road, aiming for the 'Private Drive Please Drive Slowly' sign. To the left is a footpath. Go up this track, then take the path to the left of the gate to Stanton Farm. Climb a hill, taking the path to the right when the main track bears left. At the brow go through the gate to the right and follow the path towards a line of trees. Go downhill, eventually reaching Toll Cottage.

3 Take the lane ahead, passing Broadgate Close. At the Northrepps village sign and a T-junction, turn left onto Church Street, keeping left. Pass the Foundry Arms and look for the phone box and bus stop, beyond which lies Craft Lane.

4 Turn right along Craft Lane, using the pavement until a sign marks this as a 'quiet lane' for walkers. After 700yds (640m) there is a Paston Way sign on your left. Take this through the woods, and bear left when it becomes a track to Hungry Hill farm.

5 At the lane next to the farm, turn left. After a few paces go right, following 'Circular Walk Paston Way' signs. Follow this gravel track towards the radar scanner installation.

6 Keep left where the track bends towards the radar tower, following the footpath signs. The path descends through woods, passing under a disused railway bridge before meeting the main road. Cross this, then turn left to walk on the pavement for a few paces before turning right along Coast Road.

7 Go down the steep ramp to your right to arrive at a concrete walkway. Up to your left you will see the remains of fallen houses in the crumbling cliffs. Follow the walkway (or you can walk on the sand, if you prefer) until you reach a slipway for boats. To the left of the slipway is a zig-zag pathway.

8 Follow this upwards to the top of the cliffs. The car park is just ahead of you.

WHAT TO SEE Edwin Lutyens (1869–1944) was perhaps best known for the Cenotaph in London, and the Indian capital city of New Delhi. He designed a number of buildings in Overstrand including The Pleasaunce (1897) and Overstrand Hall (1899).

WHERE TO EAT AND DRINK The Cliff Top Café, near the car park, is handy for snacks. The Foundry Arms in Northrepps serves pub food, real ale and coffee.

WHILE YOU'RE THERE Felbrigg Hall is a 17th-century house owned by the National Trust. Besides the house, there are waymarked woodland and lakeside trails, and a traditional walled garden with a dovecote and an orangery.

Overleaf: Fishing boats pulled high and dry on the beach at Cromer (Walk 9)

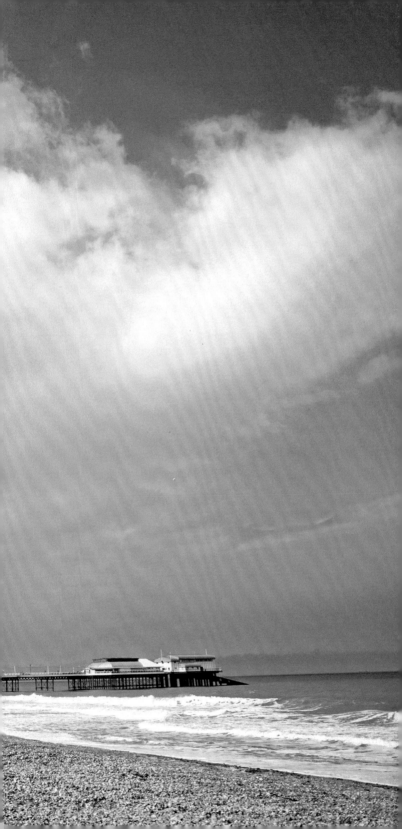

From Overstrand to Cromer

DISTANCE 4 miles (6.4km)   MINIMUM TIME 1hr 45min

ASCENT/GRADIENT 295ft (90m) ▲▲▲   LEVEL OF DIFFICULTY ✚✚✚

SEE MAP AND INFORMATION PANEL FOR WALK 8

An heroic lifeboatman and delicious crabs are just two things that have made Cromer famous. The Royal National Lifeboat Institute's Henry Blogg was an old man when he died in 1954, but anyone reading about his exploits in plucking imperilled sailors from the treacherous sea will wonder how he managed to cheat death for so long. His bravery is legendary, and he was awarded more medals and commendations than any other lifeboatman in the British Isles. Hundreds of sailors owed him their lives. You can learn more about Blogg at the Henry Blogg Museum in Cromer.

Cromer crabs, said to be the best in the country, are caught on long lines from little clinker-built boats that chug out to sea regardless of the weather. Once the pots are out, the fishermen must collect them the following day, whether a gale is raging or not. Tractors haul the boats to and from the water's edge, and watching them makes for an interesting diversion.

It's almost impossible to get lost on this walk. Start in the car park and walk to the flagpole. In the corner of the car park is a gate leading to the cliff path. This is part of the Paston Way. Follow this past the golf course, which begins at Point **A**, where you will be able to see your destination – Cromer Pier. It is important to keep to the path at all times – too far to the right and you will fall over the cliffs, while going too far to the left will put you at risk from flying golf balls.

The path goes up and down a lot. When you reach the lighthouse, Point **B**, at the end of the golf course, the path drops steeply. Eventually it becomes paved and you reach the first houses. Follow signs to the seafront, passing the monument to Blogg and a tiny garden, Point **C**. When the footpath ends, cross the street and turn right onto Brunswick Terrace, a pathway with railings.

Then go straight along East Cliff, passing St Peter and St Paul's Church (originally 15th-century, but restored in 1862) on your left. Go right down Jetty Street to the pier, Point **D**, which was built in 1900 to replace one lost in 1895. Walk down the ramp to the beach, turn right and walk for about 2 miles (3.2km) until you arrive at Point **8** on Walk 8.

Right: The imposing spire of Norwich Cathedral (Walk 10)

Norwich's Castles and Hills

DISTANCE 4.5 miles (7.2km)	**MINIMUM TIME** 2hrs 15min
ASCENT/GRADIENT Negligible ▲▲▲	**LEVEL OF DIFFICULTY** ✦✦✦

PATHS Pavements and footpaths

LANDSCAPE City buildings

SUGGESTED MAP AA Leisure Map 30 Norwich & The Norfolk Broads

START/FINISH Grid reference: TG229084

DOG FRIENDLINESS Dogs should be kept on lead

PARKING Chantry, Theatre Street; or Forum multi-storey, Bethel Street

PUBLIC TOILETS Plenty around city, including within the Forum

When William the Conqueror arrived in 1066, Norwich was already an important borough and the largest provincial city in England, with its own mint, a thriving market and some light industry. The castle was started in 1067, with a stone keep added in the first half of the 12th century. The Church was not long in recognising the city's importance and Norwich became the religious centre of East Anglia in 1096, when work began on a cathedral and priory.

By the 14th century, the main part of the city was encased in thick walls, guarded by gates and towers, which meant that access could be restricted – anyone who entered had to pay a toll. By the 15th century, Norwich was the largest walled city in Europe (its 2.5-mile/4km wall enclosed an area greater than that of the City of London) and the most important centre for worsted cloth in the country.

A 16TH-CENTURY STRUGGLE

Rebellion came to Norwich in July 1549 after angry serfs destroyed fences that had been erected to enclose common land. One who sympathised with the rebels' plight was Robert Kett, a wealthy yeoman farmer who, despite his own privileged position, agreed to their demands and offered to lead them. Along with 16,000 rebel followers, Kett set up camp on Mousehold Heath, just to the northeast of Norwich. After negotiations between the rebels and the city authorities failed, Kett used this as a base from which to storm the city. The rebels successfully fought off the government troops, led by the Marquess of Northampton, who were initially sent to quell the uprising. However, they were defeated a month later, and around 3,000 rebels are believed to have died in the final battle at Dussindale, just north of the walled city. Robert Kett was captured the following day. Following imprisonment in the Tower of London, he was tried for treason and hanged from the walls of Norwich Castle on 7 December, 1549.

Left: The cobbled square at Elm Hill, Norwich (Walk 10)

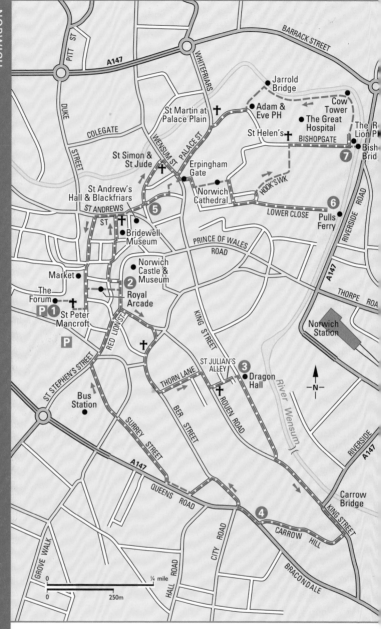

① Start at the tourist information centre, housed in the modern Forum. Cross Millennium Plain to visit St Peter Mancroft Church (1430). Leave by the south door and turn left down Hay Hill and left onto Gentleman's Walk, then right down the art

nouveau Royal Arcade (1899). From the end of the arcade continue a few yards up Arcade Street to reach Castle Meadow.

② Turn right at the castle and left along Farmers' Avenue by the Bell

Hotel. Turn right at the top onto Golden Ball Street, past St John the Baptist Timberhill Church. Go left into Ber Street, and left downhill along Thorn Lane. Turn right along Rouen Road, then left into St Julian's Alley.

❸ At the bottom turn right into King Street, admiring Dragon Hall directly opposite, and continue past Wensum Lodge on the left, St Etheldreda's Church on the right and then the Novi Sad Friendship Bridge on the left to reach Carrow Bridge just off to the left. Continue uphill past the junction and turn right up Carrow Hill to climb to a tower and section of city wall.

❹ Turn right into Bracondale and bear right again at Ber Street, then go left into Finkelgate, right on St Catherine's Plain. Go right along Surrey Street, across traffic lights and past the bus station to St Stephen's Street. Turn right and continue along Red Lion Street, finally reaching Castle Meadow again to visit the Castle Museum. From Castle Meadow, opposite the castle entrance, walk down steps to Davey Place, then turn right along Castle Street to reach London Street. Go left down Swan Lane, then right and left at Bedford Street into Bridewell Alley. with Bridewell Museum to your right.

❺ Turn right into St Andrews Street to see St Andrew's Hall and Blackfriars, part of a Dominican friary. Veer left onto Princes Street, where Garsett House (1589) is said to have been built from timbers salvaged from the Spanish Armada. Turn left at the junction with Redwell Street,

by St Peter Hungate, and walk down cobbled Elm Hill, admiring 15th-century Pettus House. Walk down Towler's Court, to see plaques marking parish boundaries.Continue along Elm Hill to the Church of St Simon and St Jude, and then turn right into Wensum Street and Tombland and the memorial to World War I heroine Edith Cavell. Turn left to go through the Erpingham Gate and head for the cathedral. When you have finished exploring it and have seen Cavell's grave at the southeast side of the cathedral, walk through the cloisters and along Lower Close (the cathedral grounds' main thoroughfare) to Pulls Ferry.

❻ Return to Lower Close then turn right on Hook's Walk, by playing fields. At Bishopgate turn right, with the Great Hospital and St Helen's Church on your left. At the end of Bishopgate is Bishop Bridge, built in 1340.

❼ Retrace your steps over the bridge and turn right by The Red Lion, following the Riverside Walk to Cow Tower (1380). Follow the river path and where it forks just before the Jarrold footbridge, go left to the 13th-century Adam and Eve pub. Pass Bishop's Palace Gate and St Martin at Palace Plain, where the dead of Kett's rebellion of 1549 are buried. At the end of Palace Street, turn left into Tombland, and directly opposite Erpingham Gate turn right into Tombland Alley and right onto Princes Street. At St Andrews Street, turn right. Turn left into Exchange Street at the traffic lights, then right again at the Market and back to the Forum.

WHILE YOU'RE THERE The Bridewell Museum focuses on Norwich life and history. More local history can be found in the Norwich Castle Museum and Art Gallery, which also displays paintings by the famous Norwich School of artists.

The Boudicca Way at Caistor St Edmund

DISTANCE 6.25 miles (10.1km)	**MINIMUM TIME** 3hrs

ASCENT/GRADIENT 279ft (85m) ▲▲▲   **LEVEL OF DIFFICULTY** +++

PATHS Paved road, permissive and public footpaths, several sets of steps

LANDSCAPE Rolling farmland and an archaeological site

SUGGESTED MAP AA Leisure Map 30 Norwich & The Norfolk Broads

START/FINISH Grid reference: TG232032

DOG FRIENDLINESS Dogs must be on lead in Roman town

PARKING South Norfolk Council and Norfolk Archaeological Trust car park at Roman fort (free)

PUBLIC TOILETS None on route

When the Romans invaded Britain, they built arrow-straight roads, established well-run, prosperous towns and developed industries like tile-making, salt production and potteries. But not all the local tribes were pleased to be part of the Roman Empire.

REBEL QUEEN

One rebel was Boudicca, who had been married to King Prasutagus of the Iceni. The trouble started when Prasutagus died in AD 60. He was barely cold in his grave before the Roman procurator's men arrived to grab property and money, and troops appeared to impose military law. One Roman insulted Boudicca, who responded with anger, and in retaliation was flogged and her daughters raped. News of this outrage spread like wildfire throughout East Anglia and the revolt was born. Her headquarters are said to have been at or near Venta Icenorum at Caistor.

Contemporary accounts tell us that Boudicca was tall, with fierce eyes and a strident voice. She had a mane of tawny hair that tumbled to her waist and she wore a striking multicoloured tunic, a gold neck torc and a cloak held by a brooch. Female rulers were not unknown to the Iceni and they quickly rallied to her fiery speeches of rebellion and revenge. Other tribes joined the throng as Boudicca's army moved against the Romans, carrying huge shields and wearing their best battle gear.

From Venta Icenorum to Colchester they marched, probably using the recently completed Roman road. The army grew until it was 100,000 strong, all angry and determined to exact revenge on their hated oppressors. Meanwhile, Colchester was wholly unprepared for the attack, because the civilians had been assured there was nothing to worry about – they had well-trained Roman soldiers to defend them. But as soon as the garrison spotted the enormous, vengeful throng, they abandoned their posts and fled for safety inside the temple of Claudius. The civilians were left to fend for themselves. A massacre followed of the most shocking magnitude. No one was spared and as many as 20,000 were killed. The wooden town was burned to the ground and the stone temple fell two days later.

Boudicca then moved on to London and St Albans, where the bloodshed continued. The Roman general Suetonius marched to meet her and the two forces met near St Albans. Suetonius' well-trained military machine was outnumbered by the Britons, but reports say that the Romans destroyed 80,000 of the larger force – an appalling number of dead for any battle. Boudicca probably poisoned herself after the defeat, but her legend lives on. This walk follows some of the 36-mile (58km) footpath named in her honour.

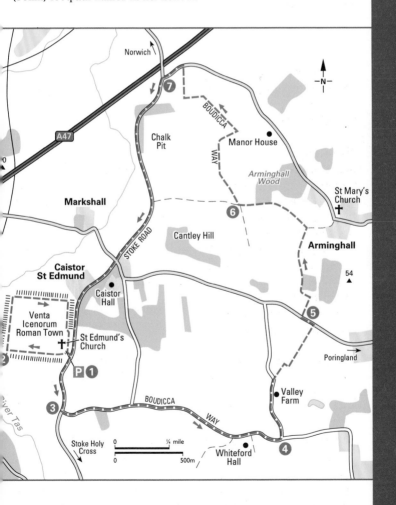

1 The first part of the walk follows the marked circular trail around Venta Icenorum, so go through the gate next to the notice board at the car park. The trail is marked by red and white circles. Climb a flight of steps, then go down six to reach the huge bank that protected the town, with a deep ditch to your left. Now head west, towards the River Tas.

2 Turn right by the bench, past fragments of old walls, then right again when you reach a longer section of wall, still following the trail markers. Go through a gate, then walk along the side of the bank with more wall to your right. Go up the steps, then descend again to the ditch on the eastern edge of the town. Go past St Edmund's Church and when you reach the car park, go through it. Cross the road, go through the gate opposite, then turn right, keeping to the broad sward between the edge of the field and the road. You are now on the Boudicca Way.

3 Just after the brick cottages take the tiny unmarked lane to your left, still keeping to the permissive path sward beside the road until the top of the hill. Continue straight past the next junction and keep walking until you pass Whiteford Hall.

4 Turn left onto Valley Farm Lane. After the farm, look for the footpath sign with a Boudicca Way marker to your right. Take this and keep to your right, along the side of a hedge. Jig right, then immediately left, and keep walking until you reach a paved lane. Turn left and then look for another footpath with a sign pointing to your right.

5 Take the footpath, and follow the markers down a hill and up the other side. It's important to keep to the footpaths here, because there are plenty of signs indicating private property. At the top of the field, take the left-hand path through the woods, continuing to follow the yellow markers for the Boudicca Way.

6 At a four-way junction, go right across a field, still on the Boudicca Way. Continue around a chalk quarry until you see a gate to the right. Follow the path straight across the field. Turn left onto Arminghall Lane.

7 At the T-junction, go left using the gravel path and the verges. Descend a hill into the village of Caistor St Edmund, and follow signs for the Roman town, passing 17th-century Caistor Hall to your left. You can avoid the last short stretch of road by going through the churchyard once more back into the car park.

WHERE TO EAT AND DRINK The Wildebeest Arms in nearby Stoke Holy Cross has a family restaurant and offers bar meals as well as selling official leaflets about the Roman site. It has an attractive seating area outside. The Stoke Holy Cross post office also sells information leaflets, drinks and confectionery.

WHAT TO SEE The wild flowers are worth seeking out. Between June and September look for common knapweed, which has hairy pink flowers and was once used to treat sore throats. Common mallows are also pink, have a thick, round stem and large reddish-mauve flowers. Also look for viper's bugloss, a member of the borage family, which has spiky, purplish-violet flowers.

Pulham Market to Pulham St Mary

DISTANCE 5.5 miles (8.8km)	MINIMUM TIME 2hrs 30min

ASCENT/GRADIENT 98ft (30m) ▲▲▲   LEVEL OF DIFFICULTY ✦✦✦

PATHS Country lanes and paths

LANDSCAPE Farmland and meadows

SUGGESTED MAP OS Explorer 230 Diss & Harleston

START/FINISH Grid reference: TM197863

DOG FRIENDLINESS Dogs should be kept on lead across farmland

PARKING Pulham Market, at car park on Falcon Road

PUBLIC TOILETS None on route

In 1915 the name Pulham was known to every schoolchild interested in aircraft, because it was the home of the great airships that were used to attack German shipping in World War I.

PULHAM PIGS

Competing with the huge German Zeppelins that were terrorising the North Sea coast, some of the airships were over 600ft (183m) long, with gondolas slung precariously underneath them. The gondolas bristled with guns and bombs, and brave crews flew these machines over the North Sea and harassed enemy U-boats. Because of their shape, they were known as Pulham Pigs. You will see one of them depicted on the Pulham St Mary village sign. The Pigs were stabled at a large site to the south of the village.

When the war ended, some of the airships were retained and one, the *R34*, completed the first ever there-and-back-again transatlantic air journey in 1919 (from East Fortune in Scotland to Mineola, New York). The gigantic *R33* broke away from its mooring in 1925, carrying some of its crew with it. The hapless men were carried out across the North Sea before they could complete enough emergency repairs to begin a homeward journey. Fortunately, 29 hours after the disaster, the ship limped back to Pulham, where it was safely secured and its crew were given a heroes' welcome.

AN OLDER HISTORY

The Romans decided this fertile valley was a good place to farm and there has been almost continuous settlement here ever since. Pulham St Mary Magdalene was granted a charter to hold a weekly market in 1249 and the villagers must have been relieved to change the name to Pulham Market, to avoid confusion with nearby Pulham St Mary the Virgin.

The grandeur of the Church of St Mary Magdalene, with its handsome arch-braced roof, is an indicator of the wealth of the village in the 15th century. In the 17th century the Puritan cloth merchant William Pennoyer bequeathed money to the village school, now the Pennoyer Centre, celebrating local history.

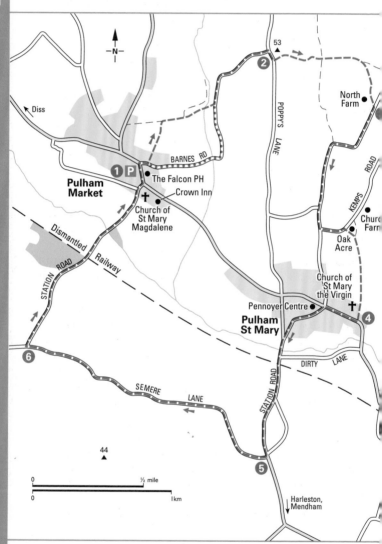

① Turn left out of Falcon Road and walk a few paces up the main street, then turn right into Barnes Road and look for the waymarked footpath on your left. Pass apple orchards and

Pulham Market Bowls Club, then continue straight ahead on a narrow path between the bowling green and a house. Cross a footbridge to enter a field, and turn right at a junction of paths. After 200yds (183m) the path divides; leave the main trail and fork right on a narrow path which runs downhill. Stay on this path as it crosses fields and a footbridge, then passes through woods and climbs some steps to return to Barnes Road. (Alternatively, you could just stay on Barnes Road to this point from the start of the walk.) Turn left and walk along Barnes Road to the junction with Poppy's Lane and Duck's Foot Road.

2 Turn right on Poppy's Lane, and after a few paces look for the wooden public footpath sign to your left. The path runs along the side of a ditch, with wide, open fields on either side. Here in this immense space you can see, and be seen, for miles. The path bears right and you head to the outbuildings of North Farm.

3 At North Farm, walk down the lane to your right on North Green Road, a meandering road that offers great views of the stocky tower of St Mary Magdalene across the fields. Pass thatched cottages and barn conversions before taking the first turning to your left, Kemps Road. Just before Oak Acre cottage, where the road bends, take the footpath to the right, which hugs a hedge for a short distance then forks half-right through the centre of a field. Go through a hedge and across a stile, keeping to the right-hand side of a meadow. Cross another stile and make your way along the backs of houses until you come out by the side of the Church of St Mary the Virgin.

4 Emerging from the church, turn right to enter Pulham St Mary and fork left by the Pennoyer Centre and village sign. At the end of the road, fork left along Station Road. Continue straight on past Dirty Lane – so named because the sewage works were once housed here. Cross a bridge over the brook and continue along Station Road for about 700yds (640m).

5 At Semere Lane, turn right and follow this narrow lane for 1.25 miles (2km) until it meets Station Road (a different one from that in Pulham St Mary).

6 At Station Road, turn right, crossing the disused railway and passing the old station. You are now back in Pulham Market, where you will see the handsome 15th-century tower of St Mary Magdalene. From here, return to the car park.

WHERE TO EAT AND DRINK In Pulham Market, The Falcon has an outdoor seating area and serves home-cooked food. The Crown Inn is about 400 years old and also serves food. The cafe at the Pennoyer Centre is open Monday to Saturday, 9.30–2.30, serving light lunches, speciality coffees and home-made cakes.

WHAT TO SEE In Pulham St Mary, Pennoyer's School dates from the 1670s and was built into the 1401 chapel of the Guild of St James. Closed in 1988, it is now the Pennoyer Centre, celebrating local history.

WHILE YOU'RE THERE Harleston, to the southeast, is a good point from which to explore the lovely countryside around the River Waveney. Harleston is also famous for its rose nurseries, and 2 miles (3.2km) further on, the little village of Mendham is the birthplace of the painter Alfred Munnings (1878–1959). To the south is Diss, with its wide mere and smattering of Victorian, Georgian and Tudor houses.

A Scenic Circuit from Blickling Hall

DISTANCE 6.5 miles (10.4km)	MINIMUM TIME 3hrs

ASCENT/GRADIENT 98ft (30m) ▲▲▲   LEVEL OF DIFFICULTY ✦✦✦

PATHS Paved lanes and some footpaths

LANDSCAPE Stately house grounds and pretty agricultural land

SUGGESTED MAP AA Walker's Map 21 North Norfolk Coast

START/FINISH Grid reference: TG176285

DOG FRIENDLINESS Dogs must be on lead in grounds of hall

PARKING Blickling Hall car park on Aylsham Road (free for NT members)

PUBLIC TOILETS Visitor centre at Blickling Hall; also in Aylsham town centre

For the walker, Blickling Hall is probably the best of the many National Trust properties found in Norfolk. The River Bure meanders pleasantly to the north of its grounds, which are full of shady, mature trees; there is a quiet lake to stroll around and the grounds are full of fascinating buildings and monuments.

A CHEQUERED HISTORY

The ancient manor of Blickling once belonged to King Harold, who built the first house here. He was defeated at Hastings by William the Conqueror in 1066, who seized Blickling for himself, then passed it to a man who later became Bishop of Thetford. The manor remained in the hands of successive bishops until it passed to a line of soldiers. One of these, Nicholas Dagworth, built a moated house here in the 1390s. Eventually Blickling came into the possession of Sir John Fastolf, widely believed to be the inspiration for Shakespeare's Falstaff, and then passed to the Boleyn family, where it remained until Anne Boleyn's dramatic fall from grace. Blickling came into the hands of the Hobart family in 1616.

The Hobarts made drastic changes, almost completely rebuilding the house between 1618 and 1629. Instead of following the contemporary craze for new Classical architecture, the Hobarts remained firmly traditional, and as a result the house is one of the finest examples of Jacobean architecture in the country. It was designed by Robert Lyminge, who also built Hatfield House, in Essex. The building is constructed of brick with stone dressings, and has a pair of handsome corner towers. The landscaped park dates from the 18th century.

FROM RUSSIA WITH LOVE

Blickling is a veritable treasure house. Perhaps its most famous acquisition is the magnificent tapestry that hangs in the Peter-the-Great Room. This belonged to John Hobart, who was described by Horace Walpole as 'painfully transparent'. He therefore appears an odd choice to appoint as Ambassador to Catherine of Russia, but to Russia he went and he seems to have made a success of his posting. It was during this sojourn that he bought the remarkable tapestry depicting the Tsar prancing along on his horse, with the carnage of Poltava in the background.

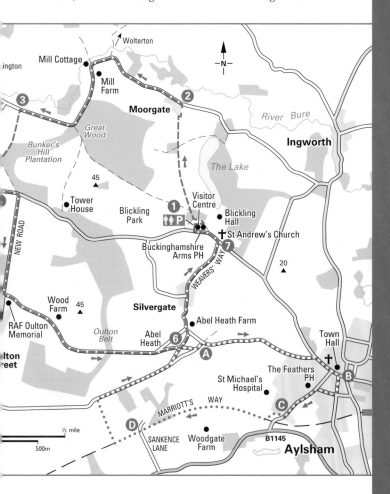

1 Go towards the National Trust visitor centre and take the gravel path to its left, past the Buckinghamshire Arms. Continue up the drive, forking right at the tree with a bench around its trunk, and go through the revolving gates into Blickling

Park. Keep ahead at a fork and follow the Weavers' Way, eventually to go through a gate into The Beeches. Continue ahead at a crossing of paths along the right-hand field edge. On nearing a house, follow the path right, then left to a lane.

2 Turn left at the lane, following its winding path until you pass Mill Cottage, complete with mill pond, on your right, and Mill Farm on your left. The mixed deciduous Great Wood on your left belongs to the National Trust. Leave the woods and walk through the pretty Bure Valley for about 700yds (640m) until you see a footpath on your left (although the 'Restricted Byway' sign is on the right).

3 Turn left down this track, with trees and hedgerows on either side. Go up a slope to Bunker's Hill Plantation (also protected by the National Trust), skirting around the edge of this before the footpath merges with a farm track. It eventually comes out onto a road.

4 Turn left and then right, onto New Road, which is signposted for Cawston and Oulton Street. This wide lane runs as straight as an arrow for about 0.75 miles (1.2km), before reaching a crossroads at the village sign for Oulton Street.

5 Turn left by the RAF Oulton memorial and its bench on the opposite verge. The lane starts off wide, but soon narrows to a peaceful rural track. Continue along this for 1.5 miles (2.4km), passing through the thin line of trees known as the Oulton Belt and eventually arriving at Abel Heath, a small conservation area owned by the National Trust.

6 Turn left by the oak tree, then left at the T-junction towards Abel Heath Farm. The lane winds downhill until you reach the red-brick cottages of the little hamlet of Silvergate. You are now on the Weavers' Way long distance footpath. Pass a cemetery on your right and continue until you see St Andrew's Church (partly 14th century, but mostly Victorian). Continue on until you reach the main road.

7 Turn left, passing the Buckinghamshire Arms and the pretty 18th- and 19th-century estate cottages at the park gates on your right. Continue walking until you see signs for the car park, where you turn right.

WHERE TO EAT AND DRINK There is a National Trust tea shop and restaurant in the Hall, with a children's menu. However, the house and its facilities open at differing times during the year, and are closed during the winter, so check ahead. The Buckinghamshire Arms stands just outside the main gates. It was originally built for the estate bricklayer Joseph Balls in 1693, but is now a pub that serves good food.

WHAT TO SEE Blickling Hall holds many treasures, but in particular you should not miss the grand South Drawing Room with its superb plaster ceiling; the Brown Drawing Room, which was a chapel in the 17th century; and the sumptuous Peter-the-Great Room and State Bedroom. In the grounds, look for the early 18th-century temple and fountain, and the 1782 Orangery.

WHILE YOU'RE THERE If you enjoy stately homes, then visit the medieval manor house of Mannington Hall 4 miles (6.4km) to the northwest of Blickling (see Walk 15). Its gorgeous gardens are open to the public in the summer and the hall itself is open by appointment. Even closer is Wolterton Hall, built in the 1720s for the Walpole family. Both houses are owned by Lord and Lady Walpole.

A Loop at Aylsham

DISTANCE 4.25 miles (6.8km)   MINIMUM TIME 1hr 45min

ASCENT/GRADIENT 98ft (30m) ▲▲▲   LEVEL OF DIFFICULTY +++

SEE MAP AND INFORMATION PANEL FOR WALK 13

Aylsham's name has its origins with the Saxons. A Saxon farmer named Aegel lived here, and his homestead became known as Aegel's Ham, which was later shortened to Aylsham. The village is recorded in the Domesday Book, and it is remarkable to see that the parish in the 1080s was about the same size as it is today.

Aylsham became Crown property after the Conquest and remained in royal hands until the reign of Charles I. Charles pawned it to the Corporation of the City of London, in an effort to raise some cash, and was never able to afford to redeem it. The City passed it to the Earls of Buckinghamshire, who owned nearby Blickling. It finally ended up with the National Trust, who remain its careful guardians today.

Start from Point **6**, turning right in Abel Heath and then right again (Point **A**) onto the lane that leads to Aylsham. The lane winds downhill to a 'Give Way' sign. Go right on Blickling Road, heading for the town centre and the Market Place, Point **B**. Originally medieval, it is dominated by 18th-century architecture and 12th-century St Michael's Church.

Just before the Market Place, turn right along Hungate Street. At the junction turn right into Mill Road, and proceed to The Feathers pub. Turn left and walk along the pavement until you pass St Michael's Hospital on your right. Before the road joins the B1145 there is a bridge, Point **C**. Don't go underneath it, but look for the zig-zag sloping path to the right.

Go up here to join Marriott's Way cycle path, turning right along the wide track. This eventually opens out to give splendid views over surrounding farmland. Continue through the gates near Woodgate Farm, and then keep straight ahead until you reach the double gates at the junction with Sankence Lane, Point **D**.

Go straight across the junction, and after 250yds (229m) you will see a farm track crossing the cycle path. Turn right at the waymarker and follow it across the middle of a field before emerging onto a lane. Turn right and walk back to Abel Heath and Point **6**.

Linking Stately Homes in the Bure Valley

DISTANCE 7 miles (11.3km)	MINIMUM TIME 3hrs

ASCENT/GRADIENT 164ft (50m) ▲▲▲   LEVEL OF DIFFICULTY ✦✦✦

PATHS Public footpaths, farm tracks and quiet lanes

LANDSCAPE Rolling fertile valley, conservation areas and woodland

SUGGESTED MAP AA Walker's Map 21 North Norfolk Coast

START/FINISH Grid reference: TG141320

DOG FRIENDLINESS Not allowed in gardens of Mannington Hall; permitted on lead in grounds of both houses

PARKING Visitor centre at Mannington Hall (pay at reception or honesty box if closed)

PUBLIC TOILETS Visitor centre at Mannington Hall

Deep in the lovely valley of the River Bure, which winds its way through fertile agricultural land on its way to the Broads, lie a pair of stately homes. These are Mannington Hall and Wolterton Hall, both owned by Lord and Lady Walpole. The grounds are run with a view to conservation and ecologically safe management, so they are a haven for wildlife.

MANNINGTON HALL

Mannington Hall is the older of the two houses. Licence to crenellate – to beef up the defences – was granted in 1451 to a man named William Lumner, and by 1460 a house was under construction. It was improved and partly rebuilt in the 1860s, and restored again in the 1960s. The house is a glorious sight, with a moat surrounding it on all sides. Inside the hall, there are some curious inscriptions on a door. These are a tirade against women, and warn the readers that 'A tiger is something worse than a snake, a demon than a tiger, a woman than a demon, and nothing worse than a woman'. These are thought to have been inscribed by the 4th Earl of Oxford.

The gardens of Mannington Hall are a joy to walk around, whether you prefer the ordered neatness of a formal rose garden or the jumbled confusion of wild flowers nodding in the breeze. The grounds also contain the ruins of 14th-century St Mary's Church, surrounded by fragments of statues and works of art collected by the 4th Earl. Inside the church is the plain sarcophagus he designed – his inscription tells us he was the only one he trusted to provide something suitably grand to hold his remains. However, he is not inside it. His successors buried him at nearby Itteringham.

WOLTERTON HALL

Wolterton Hall is a complete contrast. It was built by Thomas Ripley in the 1720s for Horatio Walpole, younger brother of Britain's first Prime Minister, Robert Walpole. It has been in the same family ever since. The building was abandoned in 1858 when the family moved to Mannington, but was restored in 1905 when they returned.

The two houses offer more than 20 miles (32km) of waymarked walks, linking to the Weavers' Way long distance trail and the Holt Circular Walk. This walk takes you on some of these permissive paths and footpaths around the estates.

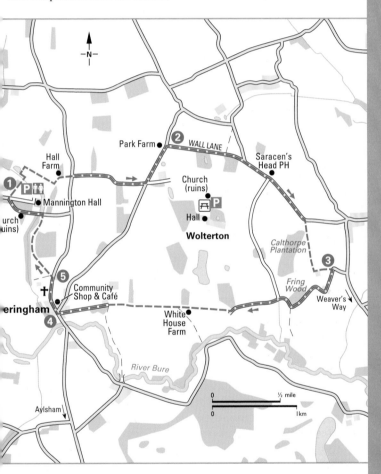

❶ From the car park head north past the information centre, following a marked trail through trees to reach a boardwalk across a wet flower meadow. This soon veers left to reach a bird hide overlooking a small lake. Turn right to follow the field edge,

to reach a junction with a track that is a public footpath (green circular sign). Turn right, where the way is marked by old oaks. Cross a stile, with Hall Farm to your left. At the end of the field go left through a gate, cross a stile at the corner of a farm building, and go right onto the driveway. Go straight across the road ahead, ascending and descending a gentle hill until you reach a second crossroads. Go left, towards Wolterton. When you reach Park Farm, turn right.

2 Follow this lane for about 1.5 miles (2.4km), passing the Saracen's Head on your left. The road is called Wall Lane and it is obvious why, with flint cobble giving way to brick wall, keeping the grounds of Wolterton safe from invaders. Wolterton Hall and the ruin of a round tower church are visible over the wall to the right. When the lane bends left, look for the footpath sign on your right. This follows the edge of two huge fields, with Calthorpe Plantation off to the right. Reaching a farm track, follow it sharp left before emerging onto a lane.

3 Turn right, then sharp right again at the next set of farm buildings.

Go left after a few paces and follow the lane around the edge of Fring Wood. When you see White House Farm, just after another small wood to the right, take the public footpath along the private drive, going through its yard and continuing ahead until you reach a stile and a farm track. Cross to the track opposite and walk through a meadow to reach Itteringham, emerging at Manor House by a junction.

4 Turn right (not sharp right) to walk uphill past the church. Continue a little further to reach a road to the left, opposite a house.

5 Take the footpath that leads diagonally left across a field towards the corner of a wood. Go through a gap in the hedge and over a stile to follow the edge of the wood. Cross another stile at the road, then turn left to walk a short distance before turning right into the car park.

WHERE TO EAT AND DRINK The Greedy Goose at Mannington Garden tea room is open when the gardens are open, and serves tea, coffee and light refreshments. The Saracen's Head, just outside the gates of Wolterton Park, serves lunches and suppers. Itteringham community shop also has a cafe, which serves drinks and light refreshments.

WHAT TO SEE For keen gardeners, Mannington Garden Shops are well worth a visit. Plants from the estates, and roses from Peter Beales, are for sale. Those who prefer wild flowers to cultivated gardens should spend a few moments near the lake, where rare and endangered species are encouraged to flourish.

WHILE YOU'RE THERE Blickling Hall(see Walk 13), often called the finest Jacobean house in England, lies 4 miles (6.4km) southeast of Mannington Hall. Baconsthorpe Castle lies 4 miles (6.4km) north, and comprises the ruins of a large 15th-century fortified manor house.

Around Wymondham Abbey

DISTANCE 5.5 miles (8.8km)   MINIMUM TIME 2hrs

ASCENT/GRADIENT 98ft (30m) ▲▲▲   LEVEL OF DIFFICULTY ✦✦✦

PATHS Town pavements, meadows, railway embankment and steps

LANDSCAPE Water-meadows, lovely old town and disused railway

SUGGESTED MAP OS Explorer 237 Norwich

START/FINISH Grid reference: TG109014

DOG FRIENDLINESS Dogs must be kept on lead in reserves

PARKING Pay-and-display car park off Market Street in Wymondham

PUBLIC TOILETS At car park

It is difficult to believe that peaceful Wymondham was once the site of a bitter dispute between its parishioners and the abbey's Benedictine monks. The two parties could not agree. They did not like the times when each other rang their bells and they did not like sharing the church. Matters came to a head in the 14th century when the monks began to build a church tower, making it clear that this was going to be for their use only. In retaliation, in 1447, the townsfolk began to build their own tower – and then installed a peal of bells. The result is a church with two towers.

The dispute dragged on for many years and was only laid to rest during the Dissolution, when the abbey buildings were destroyed and the monks expelled by Henry VIII. The people of Wymondham were allowed to keep the nave of the church, although they had to pay handsomely for it. The chancel, where the monks prayed, was demolished.

Today, the abbey church of St Mary and St Thomas of Canterbury is well worth a visit. The first thing you notice is that the grand central tower is nothing more than a shell, with the great arch that once led to the abbey buildings open to the elements. This was the monks' tower, completed in 1409. It effectively divided the church in half, and left the parishioners staring at a blank wall, while the monks enjoyed the chancel. The east wall remained blank until the screen was erected in the early 20th century. Inside, the church is a delight. There are Norman arches in the nave and an angel roof, all drawing the eye forward to the gold extravaganza of the altar screen on the east wall.

The monastery was originally founded in 1107 by William d'Albini, who also built the castle at New Buckenham (see Walk 17) and was Henry I's chief butler. The monastery was put under the stewardship of the great Benedictine abbey at St Albans, and became an abbey itself in 1448, the year after the parishioners started building the west tower.

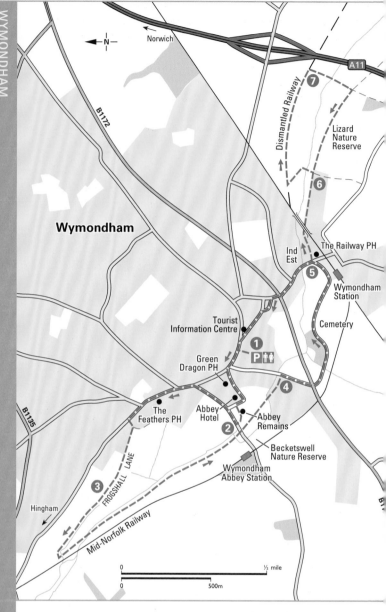

1 Exit the car park on Market Street and turn left. To your right is the Market Cross (built in 1616) and now a tourist information centre. At the bottom of the road is Church Street, leading past the chapel of Thomas Becket, founded in 1174. It is now a public library. Go past the 14th-century Green Dragon pub and the Abbey Hotel, and around the corner to reach the abbey churchyard on the left.

2 Leave the abbey churchyard through the gate by the north porch and turn right onto Becketswell Road, which becomes Vicar Street. Turn left at the war memorial, pass The Feathers pub and continue along Cock Street, then go straight across the roundabout and up Chapel Lane. A few paces will bring you to a signed track on the left called Frogshall Lane. This gravel track leads past the backs of gardens, then narrows to a grassy path, eventually reaching a kissing gate.

3 Pass through the gate. You are now entering the Tiffey Valley Project, a conservation area where grazing pastures have been restored and managed using traditional methods. Cross the meadow alongside a hedge and a fence to reach a kissing gate and a wooden footbridge across the river. Then turn left and walk along the stream bank, with views of the abbey across the meadows. Pass Wymondham Abbey station (Mid-Norfolk Railway) and cross the road to Becketswell Nature Reserve. Walk through the reserve beside the river, and continue along a surfaced path beside new housing to arrive at a bridge.

4 Turn right along White Horse Street, then cross the B1172 and head for Cemetery Lane. Walk along the lane, passing the cemetery and prize-winning Wymondham railway station, to reach an industrial estate.

5 Cross the main road and head left of The Railway pub to pass under a railway bridge.

6 After passing a row of houses, look for a path on the left leading to The Lizard, a conservation area that derives its name from an old English word for open fields. A boardwalk takes you around the edge of the meadow to where steps lead up to a disused railway embankment. Turn right, walk along the embankment and descend more steps, and walk towards a gate.

7 Go through the gate and cross a meadow, parallel to the dual-carriageway to your left, turning right when you pass a second gate. The path leads along the hedge, then crosses the meadows and exits the nature reserve by a gate. Walk along the road to return to the railway bridge. When you reach the main road, turn right up Station Road to the traffic lights, then cross and walk along Fairland Street to the left of the green, back to Market Street and the car park.

WHERE TO EAT AND DRINK The 14th-century timbered Green Dragon is the oldest pub in Wymondham and offers home-cooked food, with a walled garden in summer and a log fire in winter. Also in the town are the Cross Keys, The Heart, and Wymondham Consort Hotel.

WHAT TO SEE Look for water mint, butterbur, wild angelica, rushes and sedges in the pastures of the Tiffey Valley Project. Rail enthusiasts will enjoy the volunteer-run Mid-Norfolk Railway, opened in 1999, linking Wymondham and Dereham.

WHILE YOU'RE THERE Nearby is the attractive Georgian village of Hingham, known for its connections with the US. A rebellious rector called Robert Peck left the village in the early 17th century and founded the town of Hingham, Massachusetts. One of Abraham Lincoln's ancestors was also a Hingham man.

New Buckenham's Castle

DISTANCE 3.75 miles (6km)   MINIMUM TIME 1hr 30min

ASCENT/GRADIENT Negligible ▲▲▲   LEVEL OF DIFFICULTY ✚✚✚

PATHS Mostly country lanes

LANDSCAPE Rolling agricultural land

SUGGESTED MAP OS Explorer 237 Norwich

START/FINISH Grid reference: TM088904

DOG FRIENDLINESS Dogs should be kept on a lead from March to July on New Buckenham Common nature reserve

PARKING On village green opposite Market House

PUBLIC TOILETS None on route

In the middle of the 12th century, the powerful Norman baron William d'Albini decided that he did not much care for his castle at Old Buckenham, so he gave it to Augustinian canons and set about building himself a better one. The result was the handsome cylindrical tower at New Buckenham, 1.5 miles (2.4km) away.

TOWER FORTRESS

At first sight, you may not be impressed by the remnants of the great circular building that stands among trees on private land. It looks a bit like a giant well. But this was the first of its kind to be built in Britain and was the forerunner of such famous keeps as Pembroke, Conisbrough and Orford. Since we know from historical records that New Buckenham was built in the 1140s, we can use it to disprove the theory that round towers were a sequential advancement on square ones: New Buckenham proves that both types of fortification were apparently being built at the same time.

GRASSY BUMPS AND DITCHES

If you stand and look around, you will begin to see more of this ancient castle in the form of grassy bumps and ditches. The site was a figure of eight, with ditches all around it; parts of a 13th-century gatehouse also remain. The inner bailey – the most secure part – comprised about 2 acres (0.8ha), which was a large area to defend. It would have been protected by stone ramparts reaching 20–30ft (6–9m) high. The great tower, or keep, is in the middle of this and you will appreciate the defences would have posed a formidable obstacle to would-be attackers.

The keep itself is about 65ft (20m) across and may well once have stood about 65–70ft (20–22m) tall. It probably had four floors and was surmounted by a parapet that allowed lookouts to watch the surrounding countryside for hostile visitors. It was built with considerable care and skill. D'Albini intended his tower to be something that would last for a long time, protecting him and his household.

PARISH CHURCH

The large former barn on the road near the castle is all that remains of a chapel. This was used as New Buckenham's parish church until the 15th century, after which it was replaced by handsome St Martin's, with its lovely timber roof and effigies of the 12 Apostles.

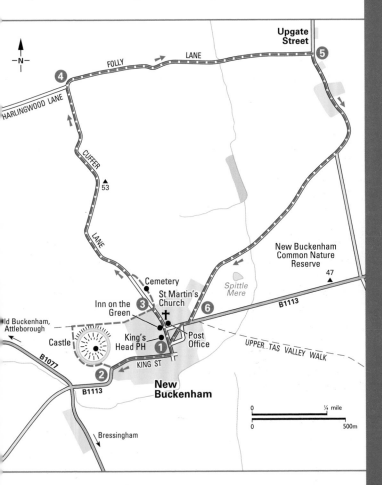

❶ Start by the former King's Head (now closed) on the village green in New Buckenham. The timber structure opposite you is the Market House, or Market Cross, which dates back to the 16th century and was raised on columnar legs in 1754. William d'Albini established a market here to attract local traders and farmers, and the tolls they paid were used to finance his new castle. Walk along Queen Street, then turn right along King Street, which becomes Castle Hill Road. When the road bends left, take the footpath to your right beside the old castle chapel, once used as a barn and now a dwelling.

2 Keep left to follow the path around the edge of the castle moat. Access to the ruins may be possible on a grassy bridge across the moat, but the gate is usually kept locked. After making a half-circuit, take the straight path that joins from the left and follow this towards the tower of St Martin's Church ahead. This soon switches fields to follow a hedgerow to the right before emerging on Cuffer Lane.

3 Cross the road to enter the long, narrow cemetery in front of you and walk through it, keeping the lane on your left-hand side. When you reach the last of the graves, pass through the gap in the hedgerow to emerge back onto Cuffer Lane. Turn right, past the village allotments, and continue walking in the same direction until you reach a sign for Harlingwood Lane.

4 Stay on this road as it bends right, becoming Folly Lane, for just over 0.75 miles (1.2km).

5 At the T-junction, turn right, then take the next right-hand turn down a surfaced track. Continue through a metal gate to enter New Buckenham Common nature reserve, an SSSI (Site of Special Scientific Interest) managed by the Norfolk Wildlife Trust. Go through another gate to continue along a narrow lane. You can sometimes see waterfowl on Spittle Mere in the scrubby meadow to your left. The water table is often high here, making the land very boggy and unsuitable for arable farming. However, it is an ideal habitat for water-loving bog plants and you will see marsh mallows, rushes and many other wetland wild flowers in season.

6 When you see a cricket pitch on your right-hand side, you are nearing the village again. Pass a children's playground, also on your right, and an information board on your left, to reach another T-junction. Turn right on the street, signed 'Norwich Road', and enter the village. After a few paces, the road forks. Take the right-hand lane, past Crawford's and Corner Cottage, until you reach the green where the walk began.

WHERE TO EAT AND DRINK The King's Head is currently closed (February 2013) but the nearby Inn on the Green serves a good range of food cooked with locally sourced fresh produce. It is open every day, lunchtime and evenings, apart from Mondays. The Gamekeeper and the Ox and Plough are two good pubs on the village green at Old Buckenham.

WHAT TO SEE There is even less of Old Buckenham Castle to see than New Buckenham, although if you happen to be on Abbey Road, you might want to see whether you can spot the remains. They comprise the remnants of a double moat, which lie in a field just to the east of Abbey Farm.

WHILE YOU'RE THERE The Church of St Mary at nearby Attleborough is well worth a visit, as its loft and huge, painted 15th-century rood screen were among few to survive the Reformation. Also look for the medieval wall painting of Moses and David. To the south is Bressingham, famous for its steam museum, where there are road and rail engines; children and adults alike can enjoy the narrow-gauge railway through the Bressingham Hall Estate.

Reepham and Salle

DISTANCE 5.25 miles (8.4km)   MINIMUM TIME 2hrs 30min

ASCENT/GRADIENT 82ft (25m) ▲▲▲   LEVEL OF DIFFICULTY +++

PATHS Field paths and trackways; beware poor signposting

LANDSCAPE Lively market town, peaceful village and rural Norfolk

SUGGESTED MAP AA Leisure Map 9 North Norfolk

START/FINISH Grid reference: TG099229

DOG FRIENDLINESS Can run free, but must be on lead on bridleway to Salle

PARKING Town car park (free) on Station Road, Reepham

PUBLIC TOILETS Town centre, clearly signposted; also in Reepham Station

Reepham has one churchyard, but three churches once graced its confines. Two of these still exist, sitting oddly side by side right in the centre of this pretty Norfolk market town. The biggest is St Michael's, dominating the Market Place with its tall tower. It is used as a hall rather than a place of worship, and has suffered from over-enthusiastic restoration. Right next to it is St Mary's, which was also ravaged by the Victorians. Parts date from the 13th century, and there is a handsome effigy of a reclining Sir Roger de Kerdiston (d.1337), and his son William. All that remains of All Saints', the third church, is a wall that survived the demolition of the rest of the building in 1796.

There is a reason why Reepham ended up with three churches in one yard, although it's not obvious. Reepham was originally more than one parish, and in William I's Domesday Book it was closely associated with the settlements at Kerdiston, Whitwell and Hackford. All Saints' belonged to Hackford, St Michael's to Whitwell, and St Mary's to Reepham and Kerdiston. This curious set-up seems to have worked remarkably well. In 1543 Hackford's church became ruinous, probably after a fire, and the parishioners moved to share with Whitwell. Eventually the parishes lost their separate identities and merged into Reepham.

REEPHAM'S RISE AND FALL

In the 19th century the town was prosperous, with its brickworks, horse-training centre, a pair of tanneries and a brewery. It had a Wednesday market and a stock fair, and was served by two fire engines and a company of the Third Norfolk Rifle Volunteers. Railway stations opened in Reepham and Whitwell in 1882, built by men with colourful names like Lumpy Ling, Spitting Joe and Sam Shirt. Unusually, the railway did not bring greater prosperity to Reepham, but served to secure its demise. Cheaper goods became available from outside and local industries began to lose customers. By the end of the century, the population had dropped from 1,800 to just 400.

The Old Brewery House in Reepham, now a hotel, was built in the early 1700s. There was once a windmill situated on Ollands Road, but the local people objected to it so much that they planted fast-growing trees nearby to prevent the wind from turning its sails. The devious ploy seemed to have worked and the miller was forced to move to a more reliable spot on the Norwich Road.

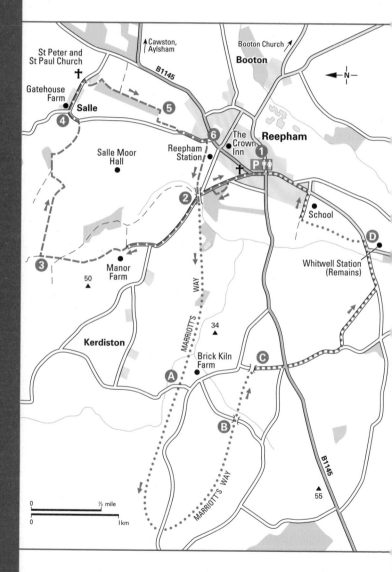

1 From the car park turn right towards the Methodist church and turn left up Kerdiston Road,

signposted 'Byway to Guestwick'. At the junction with Smuggler's Lane, take the path left into the CaSu Park.

Take the footpath ahead of you, then bear to the right each time paths meet, and you will eventually emerge through trees onto the lane again. Turn left and walk underneath a bridge.

2 Continue along the road to Manor Farm, then keep straight on to a track just before the driveway to Kerdiston Hall, where the road veers left. At first the track is gravelled, then changes to grass, which can become very muddy after wet weather. The track passes through shady woodland and passes a footpath off to the right before eventually emerging at the corner of a broader farm track.

3 Turn right to follow the farm track, with high hedges on both sides. After about 0.5 miles (800m), as the track veers a little to the right the tower of Salle church comes into view ahead. Continue past the edge of a wood before swinging to the right. When the track ends at a lane, turn left and continue to the next junction.

4 At the junction, turn right by Gatehouse Farm and walk up Salle's High Street to the church. There is a bench in the gate for the weary to rest. On leaving the church, cross the road and walk behind the two buildings opposite the church to the far left-hand corner of the village green, and turn right onto a wide green path. Walk along the edge of a field with fir trees on your right, ignoring the footpath to your left, until you reach the end of the plantation.

5 Turn right towards the road and then left along the side of a hedge. Continue until the path emerges onto a lane, and turn left until you reach a junction.

6 At the junction, take the path to the right that leads under the old railway bridge onto Marriott's Way. Walk along this cycle route past Reepham Station, complete with its platform. Continue until the path crosses a road, and you see some steps to your right, just before a steel girder sculpture. Walk down them, cross a stile, and turn right under the bridge. Walk along this lane to reach a fork, where you bear right to the car park.

WHERE TO EAT AND DRINK The Crown on Stony Lane and the Old Brewery House Hotel and King's Arms in the centre of Reepham offer bar meals and restaurants. The Crown also has a beer garden. There is a tea shop in picturesque Reepham Station, which has been restored and now has edible goods and crafts for sale.

WHAT TO SEE Salle (pronounced 'Sawl') is a gorgeous little hamlet that has won prizes for Best Kept Village. It comprises the vast St Peter and St Paul Church (one of the most impressive late medieval churches in the country), an 18th-century country house and a collection of red-brick cottages along the edge of a well-maintained green.

WHILE YOU'RE THERE In Cawston, to the east, St Agnes' Church has a 16th-century gallery with a poem about making ale. Between Cawston and Booton is Booton Common, a wild area in the care of Norfolk Wildlife Trust. Booton's Church of St Michael and All Angels is medieval, although made to look Victorian in the 19th century.

On the Marriott's Way from Reepham

DISTANCE **6.75 miles (10.9km)**   MINIMUM TIME **3hrs**

ASCENT/GRADIENT **131ft (40m)** ▲▲▲   LEVEL OF DIFFICULTY ✦✦✦

SEE MAP AND INFORMATION PANEL FOR WALK 18

NOTES On last inspection (February 2013) the Marriott's Way between Points **C** and **D** had been diverted due to badger activity damaging the track. This may revert to the original trackbed route, but for now there is an alternative route along minor roads for this stretch

The M&GN Railway was the Midlands and Great Northern, although its critics claimed the initials stood for 'Muddle and Go Nowhere'. These days the trains go nowhere at all on this line, but for walkers the closing of this particular stretch was a great boon, because it now forms the basis of the 21-mile (34km) Marriott's Way. This long distance footpath was named after William Marriott, the M&GN's first chief engineer.

At Point ❷ look for the stile on the left of the street just after the bridge. Climb over and go up the steps to Marriott's Way Thelmthorpe Link. Turn right along the track, now part of the National Cycle Network.

After about 1.25 miles (2km) the path runs under a bridge at Point **A** near Brick Kiln Farm, where there is one of the route's several information boards. Follow the path straight ahead until it bends south and then east. At Point **B** the track is elevated above the road, on an old Victorian brick bridge that has been reinforced with new wood and metal struts.

At Point **C** the alternative route leaves the trackbed of the old railway. Turn right here along the minor road and cross the B1145 before turning left at the junction. Go left at the next junction, and continue to pass under the bridge at Whitwell Station at Point **D**.

Turn left along the track immediately after the bridge and, ignoring the steps to the left back up to the Marriott's Way, walk along this grassy track (which can be very muddy, especially in winter or after rain) until you have school playing grounds to your right. Meeting another track that runs downhill towards some farm buildings, turn right and continue, slightly uphill, until you reach the school buildings. The track becomes grassed and then a paved lane with houses. At the end of the lane turn left, staying on the left-hand side of the road to walk on the pavement. At the clock shop go straight ahead up Station Road to return to the car park.

Holt Country Park

DISTANCE 4.5 miles (7.2km)   MINIMUM TIME 2hrs

ASCENT/GRADIENT 197ft (60m) ▲▲▲   LEVEL OF DIFFICULTY ✦✦✦

PATHS Forest paths, tracks across fields, some paved lanes

LANDSCAPE Forest and woodland, meadow and farmland

SUGGESTED MAP AA Walker's Map 21 North Norfolk Coast

START/FINISH Grid reference: TG082376

DOG FRIENDLINESS Dogs can run free

PARKING Country park visitor centre signposted off B1149

PUBLIC TOILETS At visitor centre

The historic Georgian town of Holt is the thriving hub of North Norfolk, and preserves that charming feel of a small country town. Although bought in 1979 by North Norfolk District Council to set up as Holt Country Park, records dating back to the 1700s show that the land south of the town was once a racecourse, with members of the nobility competing at race meetings for the 'Town Plate'. Now the 104 acres (42ha) of park is an area of mature woods next to the heathland of Holt Lowes, with the River Glaven nearby.

TREES OF LIFE

The woods are a haven for wildlife as well as a recreational resource, and are maintained as sustainable working woodland. There are more than 30 different species of tree here, including Scots pine, silver birch and oak, with management aimed at increasing the proportion of native broadleaf trees.

The visitor centre provides lists of the flora and fauna you can see in the park. At dawn or dusk, you're very likely to catch glimpses of red deer, muntjac deer or red fox, while at dusk you may have pipistrel and noctule bats flitting about above you. At any time of day you're fairly certain of seeing grey squirrels. Summer is a wonderful time when butterflies are in abundance, including red and white admiral, painted lady and purple hairstreak.

There are a number of circular trails in the park itself, and a longer one out to Hempstead and back, which this walk follows. The circular trail waymarkers are green and yellow, and are generally well maintained – which can be a blessing when the footpaths can start to disappear under burgeoning vegetation in early summer.

Visitors will note that ash dieback disease has been confirmed in the park, and while it is harmless to humans, it is important that you follow Forestry Commission advice by cleaning thoroughly any shoes, boots and clothing worn here before visiting another country site.

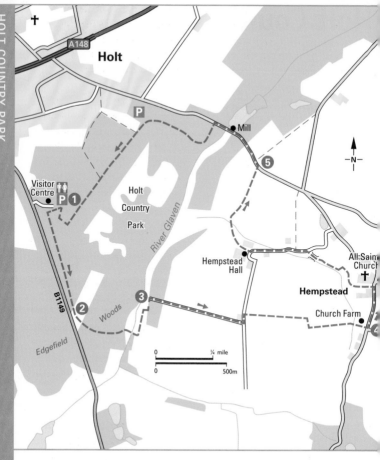

Holt

Holt Country Park

Visitor Centre

P

Mill

River Glaven

Hempstead Hall

All Saints Church

Hempstead

Church Farm

Woods

Edgefield

—N—

0   ¼ mile
0   500m

1 The walk begins at the country park car park. There are four waymarked walks through the country park itself. Follow the blue route through the pines until you pick up the green and yellow circular walk markers. The route takes you along a footpath that runs parallel to the B1149, but is shielded from it by trees. In this part of the forest you can expect to see Corsican and Scots pine, which you can tell apart by the fact that the needles on the Corsican pine have a twist and are much longer than those of the Scots pine.

2 The path crosses a stile through a clearing and leads downhill until you leave the forest and enter a meadow. Bear left, following the path, and cross a river into another meadow with woods to the right. Continue with the river to your left.

3 Follow the footpath sharp right to climb a hill, emerging onto a farm track. This ultimately leads to a barn, just past which you jig left, then right, and continue walking east along a field-edge path known as the Holt-Mannington Walk. Go right at the end of a field and then turn left after a few paces until you reach a holly bush. Cross the stile, which takes you through the hedge. The path then leads through the centre of a field and is easy to follow. The track ends in a T-junction at Church Farm (as you walk past, look into its carefully tended garden to admire the ornamental bridge).

4 Turn left along the paved lane, and then go left when you see All Saints' Church, which has a thatched apsidal end. The footpath is marked 'Holt Country Park Walk'. Enter a scrubby meadow that can be full of nettles and thistles. The path meanders, and the only way to make sure you are going in the right direction is to look for the markers. Eventually you cross a tiny wooden footbridge and meet a paved lane. Following this lane to the left will take you to Hempstead Hall, which has won prizes for farming in an environmentally sensitive manner. As you pass through the farmyard, with its densely populated duck pond, look for a stile on your right. Cross the stile and walk through a neat meadow inhabited by walker-friendly donkeys and ponies. After the meadow, cross another stile, bear right up a grassy hill and then left by the oak tree at the top. At the end of this farm track meet a lane and turn left.

5 The lane enters a wooded area, crosses the River Glaven and climbs a hill. When you reach the summit, just past a triangular warning sign for deer (facing away from you), look for the footpath sign on your left. When you reach it, turn into the wood and follow the green and yellow circular trail markers along the forest trail that runs parallel to the road. Turn left onto the track into the car park (but not the one you are parked in) and follow the path leading from the far end. Take the path branching right, just past a litter bin. Where the path forks, go right, looking for the gate and circular walk markers. Follow a straight track, continuing to follow the green and yellow markers back to the car park.

WHERE TO EAT AND DRINK The King's Head in the centre of nearby Holt serves bar meals. There is also an excellent greengrocer and a supermarket for supplies if you want to enjoy the picnic facility in the country park. In high summer, an ice cream van can be found near the park's visitor centre.

WHAT TO SEE Most trees in the country park are pines – firs, spruces and larches – but also look for native oak and introduced rhododendrons. When you find the oaks, look for evidence of gall wasps. These insects induce a variety of growths on oaks, which are named according to their shape: marble, artichoke, oak apple and knopper galls. Resident birds include robins and goldcrests.

WHILE YOU'RE THERE Holt owes its 18th-century grandeur to a devastating fire in 1708, which destroyed much of its medieval heritage. It is best known for Gresham's School, founded in 1555 by Thomas Gresham, Lord Mayor of London. North Norfolk Railway steam trains run from Sheringham to Holt, while nearby Letheringsett has a watermill.

A Loop from Mattishall to Hockering

DISTANCE 7 miles (11.3km)   MINIMUM TIME 2hrs 30min

ASCENT/GRADIENT 131ft (40m) ▲▲▲   LEVEL OF DIFFICULTY ✛✛✛

PATHS Mostly paved country lanes

LANDSCAPE Gently rolling farmland

SUGGESTED MAP AA Leisure Map 9 North Norfolk

START/FINISH Grid reference: TG053110

DOG FRIENDLINESS Dogs should be under strict control – watch for traffic on these generally quiet lanes

PARKING At village square behind Mattishall Church on Church Plain

PUBLIC TOILETS None on route

In 1776 a young parson arrived at the village of Weston Longville and began to keep a diary. His name was James Woodforde and he continued to write his account of life in his parish until his death in 1803. These were turbulent times: the colonists were rebelling in North America, King George III suffered periodic bouts of insanity, the French Revolution was in full swing, Napoleon Bonaparte was moving across Europe and there were rebellions in Ireland. Yet none of these momentous events sully the pages of this country parson.

A PLEASURE IN SMALL THINGS

His diaries recount the daily happenings in the life of a comfortable clergyman with a great many friends and a taste for good food. From Weston Longville, he visited all his neighbours in the parishes round about and attended services in the churches you will see on this walk.

In 1778 France joined the colonies against the British and the philosopher Voltaire died, but Woodforde wrote about how his two pigs got into a beer barrel and became intoxicated to the point where they were unable to stand. His diary for 28 January, 1780 reads: 'We had for dinner a calf's head, boiled fowl and tongue, a saddle of mutton roasted on the side table, and a fine swan roasted with currant jelly sauce for the first course. The second course a couple of wild fowl called dun fowls, larks, blancmange, tarts etc, etc and a good dessert...' He went on to comment that this was his first taste of swan, but that he did not consider it spoiled by the fact that it had been killed some three weeks previously. Perhaps this was due to the 'sweet sauce' that went with it.

Woodforde's diaries went undiscovered until 1924, when they were published. The parishes that he knew have joined together to design the Eight Parishes Circular Walk, moving in the footsteps of the jolly parson as he ate and drank his way around the region.

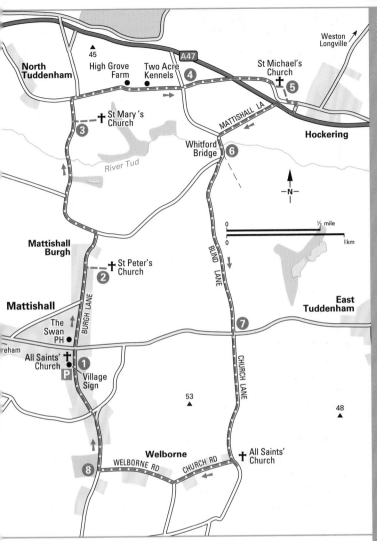

Leave the car park next to the circular village sign with four panels depicting aspects of Mattishall's history, and walk around the charming 14th-century All Saints' Church. Cross Dereham Road and head for Burgh Lane opposite. Walk up this, past the cemetery and through a residential area until you see Church Lane on your right. Walk down the lane to reach Mattishall Burgh's St Peter's Church (originally Norman, with later additions).

Leave the church and retrace your steps to Burgh Lane. Turn right and continue walking until you reach a T-junction. Turn left, following the signs to North Tuddenham. The lane narrows, and winds down a hill to go over a bridge and up the other side. Keep going straight ahead until you reach an unpaved lane on your right after about 0.75 miles (1.2km).

Turn right and follow the track to charming 14th-century St Mary's

Church, North Tuddenham. Retrace your steps to the paved lane, turn right and continue to another T-junction. Go right, along the lane signed to Hockering and Honingham. Stay on this lane past High Grove Farm and Two Acre Kennels, until you reach a crossroads.

4 Keep straight ahead along a narrow single-track lane, aiming for the battlemented tower of Hockering's St Michael's Church (early 1300s). Cross the A47 carefully, and aim for the lane opposite. There is a notice board outside the church giving details of the Eight Parishes Project and Parson Woodforde.

5 Walk through the churchyard and look for two brick buttresses. Opposite these is a gate. Go through this, and the field ahead to reach the lane. Turn left, then right and recross the A47, aiming for the lane opposite and to your right, called Mattishall Lane. Continue past a road that joins from the right to reach a bridge.

6 Cross over Whitford Bridge, and – ignoring a farm track to the left – keep left at the following junction called Blind Lane (not signed). Walk for about a mile (1.6km) until you reach a crossroads.

7 Go straight through the crossroads, walking down Church Lane until you reach Welborne. When you reach the junction, continue a few paces past the village hall to see All Saints' Church, which has a 12th-century round tower. Retrace your steps and turn left along Church Road, and then bear right at the next junction back towards Mattishall.

8 Turn right towards Mattishall at the end of Welborne Road, and keep walking until you reach Church Plain again.

WHERE TO EAT AND DRINK The Swan, in Dereham Road at the start of the walk, serves drinks only. You can put together a picnic from the bakery at Victoria Stores together with cheese, pasties and pies from Hewitts Butchers. Yaxham Mill, on the road from Mattishall to Dereham, is a restaurant in an old windmill.

WHAT TO SEE Mattishall is a charming village. The land behind the church is known as Church Plain, and has a number of 18th- and 19th-century buildings. The Old Vicarage on Dereham Road is also 18th century. Look for the Quaker House, an 18th-century Quaker chapel and farmhouse. Mattishall Hall dates from the same period.

WHILE YOU'RE THERE Visit Parson Woodforde's Church of All Saints' in Weston Longville, which dates from the 13th and 14th centuries, and remains much as Woodforde would have known it. His rectory has been rebuilt, although the pond in the grounds where he outfoxed customs men is still there. The great barn where he collected his tithes also still stands.

North Elmham and the Saxon Cathedral

DISTANCE 5.75 miles (9.2km)   MINIMUM TIME 2hrs 15min

ASCENT/GRADIENT 115ft (35m) ▲▲▲   LEVEL OF DIFFICULTY ✚✚✚

PATHS Disused railway line and paved roads, some steps

LANDSCAPE Railway track and open woodland and farmland

SUGGESTED MAP AA Leisure Map 6 North West Norfolk

START/FINISH Grid reference: TF988216

DOG FRIENDLINESS Dogs must be kept on lead on roads and in the cathedral ruins

PARKING Car park near Saxon cathedral in North Elmham village

PUBLIC TOILETS None on route

In the period often known as the Dark Ages, when Christianity was fighting to establish itself in England, the Saxons founded a cathedral at the small village of Elmham in Norfolk. This quickly became the most important religious centre in East Anglia and was the seat of bishops. It is even possible that Edmund, the early King and martyr who was murdered by Viking raiders, was crowned here. From the year AD 800, or possibly slightly earlier, the bishops of East Anglia resided in North Elmham, running their sees and managing their religious and secular affairs.

Around AD 866 the Danes arrived, and were said to have laid the place to waste, destroying not only the cathedral but the settlement too, forcing the bishops to abandon Elmham for a safer place. The see was re-established in AD 955 and a new cathedral raised (possibly on the same site), and these are the foundations that have been excavated and that can be seen today. Four years after the Norman Conquest, the see was moved again, this time to Thetford, where it remained until 1094. It was then decided that Norwich was a far more prestigious place and the see was moved once more. This move, however, was permanent and the bishop still has his cathedral (or seat) in Norwich Cathedral today.

NORMAN EARTHWORKS

The Saxon cathedral was probably a timber building – we have two separate accounts from the 13th century and both claim it was built of wood. Archaeologists have discovered post holes, indicating a fairly basic structure. Unfortunately, one Bishop Despenser raised himself a fortified manor house here in the 14th century and the foundations of the Saxon cathedral are all mixed up with those of his house. There is a huge earthwork to the northwest of the site, but this is more likely to be a Norman motte (or castle mound) than a Saxon fortification.

We may never know what the Saxon cathedral looked like, but the later Norman chapel built over it is easier to make out. The transepts were similar to those at Norwich Cathedral and the abbey at Bury St Edmund, so they must date from after the Conquest. The north doorway is also Norman. The twin towers (often referred to prosaically as 'armpit towers') are an unusual feature to be found in England, although they appear in Germany in the first half of the 12th century.

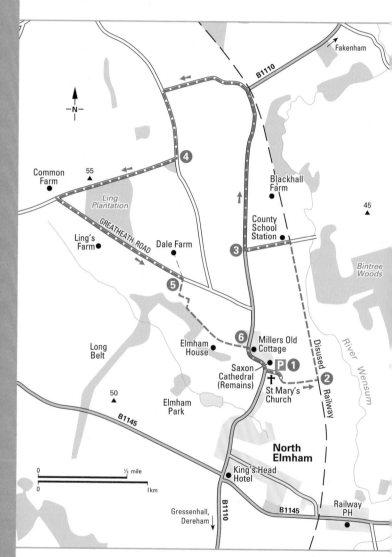

❶ Look around the site of the Saxon cathedral, then leave the way you entered. Turn left along a gravel track with Vicarage Farm and North Elmham's parish church of St Mary's to your right. The path winds downhill with hedges on either side until you reach an old bridge with a disused railway running underneath it. Cross the bridge and look for the stile immediately to your left.

❷ Walk through the gap beside the stile and descend the steps to reach the disused railway line. Turn right, and continue along the path until functional railway tracks appear. At this point the path moves away to the right, safely tucked to one side. After about 0.75 miles (1.2km) you reach County School Station. Turn left along the minor road to reach a T-junction.

❸ Turn right and follow the B1110 for about 0.75 miles (1.2km) to reach the remains of a Victorian railway bridge. Turn left, following the blue cycleway signs directing riders to King's Lynn and Fakenham. Walk on this quiet lane until you reach a T-junction. Turn left and continue uphill to reach the next junction.

❹ Turn right along a shady lane, passing pretty Ling Plantation on your left. Turn sharp left along Greatheath Road, signposted to North Elmham, to pass the other side of Ling Plantation. Walk along this lovely lane for a little more than 0.75 miles (1.2km), until you reach some scattered houses. At the end of these, take the footpath off to your right, opposite the track leading to Dale Farm on your left.

❺ Follow the footpath, a wide gravel track, around to the left behind some houses and then right, towards another plantation. Turn left along a smaller path into the woods, following the green arrows. The path follows the edge of a private wood. Emerge onto the driveway to Elmham House and come out on the B1110 by an old red telephone box and posting box. This is North Elmham's High Street. Opposite you will see Millers Old Cottage.

❻ Turn right along the High Street and walk until you see signs for the Saxon cathedral off to your left. Follow them back to the car park.

WHERE TO EAT AND DRINK There is nowhere to eat on this route, except on summer Sundays when the tea room at County School Station serves drinks and snacks. In North Elmham, the King's Head Hotel has a restaurant and beer garden, while the Railway pub serves bar meals throughout the day.

WHAT TO SEE County School Station was built in 1886 to provide a railway service to the County School and was in use until 1964. It has been carefully restored and is now a visitor centre and museum with a small cafe and picnic area. There is plenty to see, including photographs and maps.

WHILE YOU'RE THERE Gressenhall and its workhouse and Museum of Norfolk Life (see Walk 25) is about 3 miles (4.8km) to the south of North Elmham. Pensthorpe Waterfowl Park is located in Fakenham, to the north. Here you will see plenty of wading birds, ducks, swans and geese, along with woodland walks, wild flower meadows and attractive gardens.

Around the Marshes from Blakeney

DISTANCE 4.5 miles (7.2km)	**MINIMUM TIME** 2hrs

ASCENT/GRADIENT 98ft (30m) ▲▲▲   **LEVEL OF DIFFICULTY** ✚✚✚

PATHS Footpaths with some paved lanes, can flood in winter

LANDSCAPE Salt marshes, scrubby meadows and farmland

SUGGESTED MAP AA Walker's Map 21 North Norfolk Coast

START/FINISH Grid reference: TG028442

DOG FRIENDLINESS Under strict control as these are important refuges for birds

PARKING Carnser car park (pay-and-display, free for NT members), on seafront opposite Blakeney Guildhall and Manor Hotel

PUBLIC TOILETS Across road from Carnser car park

Blakeney was a prosperous port in medieval times, but went into decline when its sea channels began to silt up. While the merchants decried the slow accumulation of salt marsh and sand bars, birds began to flock here in their thousands. By Victorian times it had become such a favoured spot with feathered migrants that it became known as the place to go shooting and collecting. Some sportsmen just wanted to kill the many waterfowl, while others were more interested in trophy collecting – looking for species that were rare or little-known. The maxim 'what's hit is history; what's missed is mystery' was very characteristic of the Victorians' attitude to biological science. Many of these hapless birds ended up stuffed in museums or private collections.

NATURE RESERVE

After many years of bloody slaughter, the National Trust arrived in 1912 and purchased the area from Cley Beach to the tip of the sand and shingle peninsula of Blakeney Point. It became one of the first nature reserves to be safeguarded in Britain. Today it is a fabulous place for a walk, regardless of whether you are interested in ornithology. A bright summer day will show you glittering streams, salt-scented grasses waving gently in the breeze and pretty-sailed yachts bobbing in the distance. By contrast, a wet and windy day in winter will reveal the stark beauty of this place, with the distant roar of white-capped waves pounding the beach, rain-drenched vegetation and a menacing low-hung sky filled with scudding clouds. It doesn't matter what the weather is like at Blakeney, because a walk here is always invigorating.

Although these days we regard the Victorians' wholesale slaughter with distaste, they did leave behind them a legacy of valuable information. It was 19th-century trophy hunters who saw the Pallas'

Right: Low tide in the creek at Blakeney (Walk 23)

warbler and the yellow-breasted bunting in Britain for the first time – and they were seen at Blakeney. A little later, when the Cley Bird Observatory operated here between 1949 and 1963, the first subalpine warbler in Norfolk was captured and ringed. The Victorians' records tell us that a good many red-spotted bluethroats appeared in September and October, and any collector who happened to visit then was almost certain to bag one. In the 1950s the observatory discovered that these were becoming rare at this time of year. Today, bluethroats are regular spring visitors, but are seldom seen in the autumn. It is thought that this change over time is related to different weather patterns and indicates how climate change, even on a small scale, can dramatically effect the behaviour of birds.

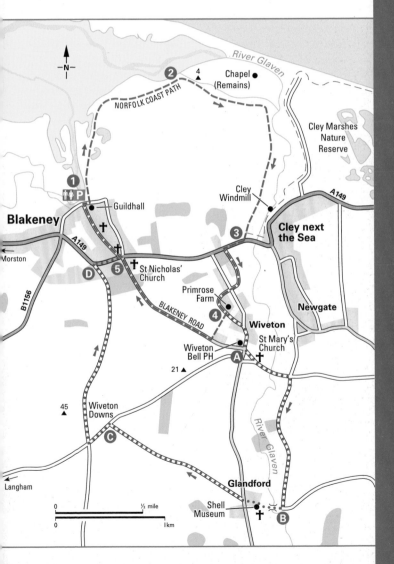

Left: Marshes at Cley next the Sea (Walks 23 and 24)

1 From the car park take the path marked Norfolk Coast Path out towards the marshes. This raised bank is part of the sea defences, and takes you all the way round to Cley. Eventually, you have salt marshes on both sides.

2 Maps older than 2005 show the path sticking closer to the coast. Over the winter of 2005–06, the course of the River Glaven, and the embankment, was moved south. This part of the walk is excellent for spotting kittiwakes and terns in late summer. Also look for Sabine's gulls, manx and sooty shearwaters, godwits, turnstones and curlews. The path leads you past Cley Windmill, built in 1810. It last operated in 1919, and now offers stylish bed-and-breakfast and self-catering accommodation. Follow signs for the Norfolk Coast Path until you reach the A149.

3 Cross the A149 to the pavement opposite, then turn right. Take the first left after crossing the little creek. Eventually you reach the cobblestone houses of Wiveton and a crossroads; go straight ahead.

4 Take the grassy bridleway track opposite Primrose Farm, to a T-junction. This is Blakeney Road; turn right along it. However, if you want refreshments before the homeward stretch, turn left and walk a short way to the Wiveton Bell. The lane is wide and ahead you will see St Nicholas' Church nestling among trees. This dates from the 13th century, but was extended in the 14th. Its two towers served as navigation beacons for sailors, and the east (narrower) one is floodlit at night.

5 At the A149 there are two lanes opposite you. Take the High Street fork on the left to walk through the centre of Blakeney village. Many cottages are owned by the Blakeney Neighbourhood Housing Society, which rents homes to those locals unable to buy their own. Don't miss the 14th-century Guildhall undercroft at the bottom of Mariner's Hill. After you have explored the area, continue to the car park.

WHERE TO EAT AND DRINK In Blakeney the Kabin sandwich bar in the car park operates between Easter and October, and sells snacks, tea and coffee. The Blakeney Hotel, Manor Hotel, White Horse and King's Arms all have restaurants and bar food. There are also several shops for picnic supplies. The Moorings Bistro serves tea and coffee as well as meals. On the walk itself you can try the Wiveton Bell.

WHAT TO SEE Blakeney Point and its marshes form one of the best birding areas in Norfolk. What you see depends on the time of year, but in the winter you can expect a huge variety of waterfowl, along with curlews, rock pipits and hen harriers. In early summer plovers and terns arrive, while high summer and autumn are the best seasons, with the potential for spotting hundreds of different species of birds.

WHILE YOU'RE THERE Morston Marshes are in the care of the National Trust and are an important site for migrating wrynecks, and icterine and barred warblers. If you have time, a boat trip out to see the seals is a rewarding experience. These endearing creatures breed and bask on the isolated sandbars to the north.

The Inland Route from Cley to Blakeney

DISTANCE 7.25 miles (11.7km) MINIMUM TIME 3hrs

ASCENT/GRADIENT 131ft (40m) ▲▲▲ LEVEL OF DIFFICULTY ✚✚✚

SEE MAP AND INFORMATION PANEL FOR WALK 23

Sir Alfred Jodrell was a model Victorian gentleman. He lived in 18th-century Bayfield House, just a mile (1.6km) to the south of Glandford, and he was greatly interested both in the area in which he lived and in natural history. He began gathering seashells in a way that was common among wealthy, enthusiastic amateurs in his day, and this collection now forms the basis of the Glandford Shell Museum. The shells are impressive and include pristine samples from all over the world. The museum is housed in a cottage built in the Flemish style.

Leave the main walk at Point ❹, continue down the lane past cottages and bear right at the T-junction. Eventually you reach a crossroads, Point Ⓐ, with St Mary's Church standing in splendid isolation on a green on one side, and the Wiveton Bell on the other. Go left, along the lane signed to Cley, crossing an attractive little bridge over the River Glaven.

After the bridge, turn right towards Glandford and its unbridged ford. The lane is one of Norfolk's best, with dog roses winding among the hawthorns and the whole place alive with the calls and rustles of nesting birds in spring. Go right at the next junction, Point Ⓑ, and cross the footbridge over the river. Because there are no cars, ducks sit happily across the road. It is worth spending a few minutes relaxing on the bench here, enjoying the peaceful gurgle of the river and the fuss of the ducks.

Glandford begins on the west bank of the river, boasting flint and red-brick houses, many with Dutch gables. St Martin's Church and the Shell Museum are on your left. At the crossroads go up the unmarked lane towards Langham, which climbs ever upwards to the Wiveton Downs, Point Ⓒ. The Downs afford splendid views towards the sea. At the junction turn left for a few paces, then turn right along the wide, open lane that will bring you to the outskirts of Blakeney. Ahead, you can spot St Nicholas' Church nestling among its chestnut trees.

When you reach the A149, Point Ⓓ, turn right, staying on the right side of the road to walk on the pavement into the village. Take the first left by the Catholic church, where you rejoin the main walk at Point ❺.

Gressenhall and the Museum of Norfolk Life

DISTANCE 8.5 miles (13.7km)   **MINIMUM TIME** 3hrs 30min

ASCENT/GRADIENT 180ft (55m) ▲▲▲   **LEVEL OF DIFFICULTY** +++

PATHS Country lanes and footpaths, can be muddy after rain

LANDSCAPE Gently rolling agricultural land

SUGGESTED MAP AA Leisure Map 6 North West Norfolk

START/FINISH Grid reference: TF975171

DOG FRIENDLINESS Lead required for short road sections

PARKING Gressenhall Farm and Workhouse – Museum of Norfolk Life; when museum is closed, at car park by bridge

PUBLIC TOILETS None on route; toilets at cafe in museum

What should be done about the poor? This was the question that vexed politicians and philanthropists in the 18th century, just as it does today. The answer in those days, however, was to build workhouses, so that people were provided with beds, clothes and food, and their waking hours were taken up with 'honest labour'.

GRESSENHALL UNION WORKHOUSE

One such institution was built at Gressenhall between 1776 and 1777, at the cost of £15,000. It was called the Union Workhouse, and was home to adults and children alike. The building is impressive – a surprising sight to appear suddenly among the trees in this pleasant countryside. It was H-plan in design, with two L-shaped extensions in the east. More buildings were added in the mid-1830s, when the Poor Law Amendment Act required workhouses to change.

Today it is an extensive and fascinating museum. Not only are there exhibitions about workhouse life, but Union Farm still works the land in the traditional way using heavy horses. There is a 1930s-style village high street with a post office, blacksmith's forge and grocer, and well-maintained gardens, including 50 acres (20ha) of unspoiled countryside with marked woodland walks and nature trails. There is also a cemetery for those who died here, and yards where men and women were separated by high walls.

Begin your day here (open daily from early March to early November), learning about what life was like in Norfolk in bygone days, and then move on to a country walk where little has changed since Union Workhouse rang with the voices of its pauper inmates.

West of Gressenhall village along the Nar Valley Way stands the tiny hamlet of Bittering. Bittering was once a much larger village gathered around a moated manor house, the remains of which are still just visible today. The hall (demolished in the 1980s) that was built to replace the manor house was once the residence of the famous anti-slavery campaigner William Wilberforce.

Nearby Little Bittering, sometimes referred to as Bittering Parva, is the site of a former medieval village that was mentioned in the Domesday Book of 1086, but which had disappeared completely by 1500. This is one of around 200 deserted villages in Norfolk that were abandoned for a variety of reasons, usually because of plague, population decrease or changes in farming practices.

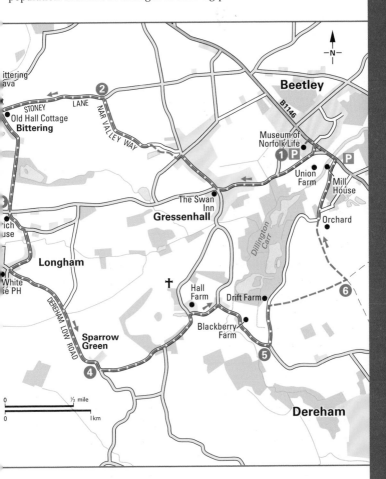

① Leave the car park and turn right onto the B1146. Take the next right, where a sign marks the Nar Valley Way, one of Norfolk's prettiest long distance footpaths. This takes you past a copse and then through Gressenhall itself. When you reach

The Swan Inn turn right along Bittering Street, past more houses, until you reach a crossroads. Turn left, following signs for the Nar Valley Way. After about 100yds (91m), take the bridleway to your right, still the Nar Valley Way. This narrow path lies between tall hedges and is like a green tunnel in summer and spring, although it can be muddy in winter It widens eventually and, after about 0.75 miles (1.2km), emerges onto a track called Stoney Lane.

2 Turn left, still following signs for the Nar Valley Way, and walk for another 0.75 miles (1.2km) to reach Old Hall Cottage at a junction and a plantation of tall trees. Turn left, leaving the Nar Valley Way. The foundations of the deserted village of Bittering Parva are to the right.

3 When you reach a crossroads and Ostrich House, follow the lane towards Longham. Stay on this lane, passing Ostrich Lane to your right, then turn right when you see a sign to the Village Hall. Pass the Village Hall and continue along this street. When you see The White Horse at Longham ahead, take a sharp left along Dereham Low Road, signposted 'Scarning'. Walk down a hill, then up the other side, with views across working land to your right.

4 Once you have passed the Sparrow Green barn conversions and a pair of silos, turn left at Park Farm Cottages, and walk for 0.75 miles (1.2km), ignoring the first lane to your right, and bearing right at the next junction. At the junction after that bear right again, following signs for Dereham, past the old cottages on your left. The road winds along a shallow valley to go over a brick bridge and pass Norfolk Herbs at Blackberry Farm.

5 Turn left along the gravel track signposted to Drift Farm (public footpath) and follow the signs uphill along a track to the right before you reach the farm itself.

6 At a crossing of paths, take the one to your left. The path runs alongside an orchard before becoming a paved track. Keep straight ahead, following the tall hedge and occasional red arrows. When you reach Mill House, turn left onto the main road. Walk along this road until you arrive at the museum on your left.

WHERE TO EAT AND DRINK There is a cafe in the museum serving teas, coffees and snacks, as well as hot meals and cold drinks. On the walk you can take a mid-way break at The White Horse at Longham, which serves home-cooked meals and real ales. The Swan Inn at Gressenhall has a beer garden and serves home-made dishes and desserts.

WHAT TO SEE The little Church of St Peter in Bittering stands on its own; it dates from the 13th century and was altered during the 15th. There was once a moated manor house close by, and although it was destroyed in the 1800s the moat is still just visible.

WHILE YOU'RE THERE Visit The Workhouse Experience inside the museum, where costumed actors bring the past to life. Children will also enjoy the woodland playground and taking a cart ride around Union Farm. The Animal Ark (formerly Norfolk Wildlife Park), just off the A1067 in the village of Great Witchingham, has rare breed farm animals as well as more exotic species including wallabies, llamas and chinchillas.

From Walsingham to Great Snoring

DISTANCE 7.25 miles (11.7km)	MINIMUM TIME 3hrs 15min
ASCENT/GRADIENT 164ft (50m) ▲▲▲	LEVEL OF DIFFICULTY ✚✚✚

PATHS Mostly country lanes

LANDSCAPE Rolling agricultural scenery with meadows and woodland

SUGGESTED MAP AA Walker's Map 21 North Norfolk Coast

START/FINISH Grid reference: TF933368

DOG FRIENDLINESS Dogs can run free along the former railway track

PARKING Pay-and-display car park in Little Walsingham

PUBLIC TOILETS At shrine and Slipper Chapel

In the 11th century, Richeldis de Faverches was lady of the manor in Walsingham. One night the Virgin Mary appeared to her in a dream and told her to build a copy of the Sancta Casa, the 'Holy House' in Nazareth where she had been living when the Angel Gabriel announced she was pregnant. Richeldis was torn between two sites for the building, but work began on one of them as soon as she had gathered supplies and labourers. Although the men worked all day, they made little progress. However, it is said that the following morning, the house on the second site had been miraculously completed. A couple of holy springs bubbled up, the sick were cured and soon Walsingham became one of the most important pilgrimage sites in the medieval world – perhaps even greater than Canterbury.

A THRIVING SITE OF PILGRIMAGE

The shrine did not remain a small house with two wells for long. As pilgrims flocked here, so did those in the service industry, and soon inns and guest houses for travellers were built. Franciscan friars and Augustinian canons built themselves priories. These were simple at first, but as more and more pilgrims arrived and left behind their pennies and their gifts, the priories became larger and more sumptuous. There was a handsome church for pilgrims to pray in and a special chapel for a statue of the Virgin, richly bedecked in jewels and fine cloth.

When the Holy Land was retaken by the Infidels after the Crusades, it was rumoured that the Virgin Mary had abandoned her original shrine and had come to live in Norfolk instead. One tale even had it that the original Sancta Casa had magically uprooted itself from Nazareth and landed at Walsingham! The shrine was visited by paupers and kings alike, and many monarchs, from Richard I to Henry VIII, came to pay homage and to ask for favours. Walsingham's future seemed glitteringly assured.

The village's success lasted for 500 years, until the Reformation. The two priories were torn down in the 1530s, so that only fragments remain, and papist practices such as worshipping statues of Mary were forbidden. Walsingham became just like any other village, and so it remained, almost forgotten by the outside world, until the 1930s, when Father Hope Patten revived the shrine. Walsingham has come full circle, and is once again a thriving pilgrimage site.

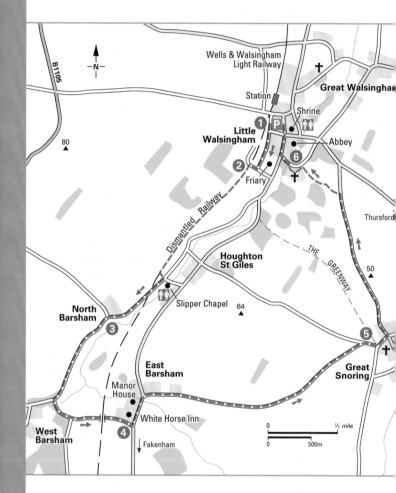

❶ Return to the main exit of the car park and turn left, soon to go down Coker's Hill. Go straight across at the junction along Back Lane. The remains of the Franciscan friary are over a flint wall to your left, incorporated into a private house. At

a T-junction, turn right uphill, then where the lane curves right, go left along the Pilgrims' Way, the route of a dismantled railway.

❷ Follow the level gravel path through open country with good views for 1 mile (1.6km). When it ends, turn left into Houghton St Giles and turn right to pass the Slipper Chapel on your left (built in the 1300s and partly destroyed during the Reformation), then continue past the former railway until you enter North Barsham.

3 At the junction, keep left, and take the lane signposted to West Barsham, to reach a junction in a shady copse. Take the lane to the left, up the hill with a fir plantation on your right. Go down a hill, past another junction to the right and more of the dismantled railway, to eventually reach the village of East Barsham.

4 Turn left at the T-junction and walk past the White Horse Inn. Just after passing a very ornate red-brick manor house, turn right into high-banked Water Lane, signed to Great Snoring. Look for partridges, yellowhammers and finches in the hedgerows.

5 At the junction, take the right-hand turn. (It is possible to take The Greenway to Walsingham shortly after this point, but be warned that it can be extremely boggy.) Continue ahead into Great Snoring with the church to your right, and turn left at the crossroads by the bus stop to quickly reach open fields again. After a mile (1.6 km), look out for an arrowed path on the left and cross a stile into a field. Follow the worn path ahead under telephone wires, which soon curves left to a gate. Continue across pasture to a further stile and turn right along a drive next to farm buildings, with the abbey ruins visible ahead. At the road, follow the path left along the back and into St Mary's churchyard.

6 Leave the churchyard via the main gate and continue along the road, turning right at the junction into Little Walsingham. To visit the Anglican shrine, turn right at the pump house, topped with a brazier that is lit on state occasions; otherwise keep ahead and then turn immediately left to reach the car park.

WHERE TO EAT AND DRINK As this is a place that anticipates large numbers of pilgrims (there is a coach park), there are a number of cafes and restaurants in the town, like The Old Bakery and Walsingham Tearooms on the High Street. The Textile Centre has a tea room, and there is a cafe at the Roman Catholic Slipper Chapel. The White Horse Inn at East Barsham serves good food.

WHAT TO SEE The grounds of privately owned Walsingham Abbey – which contain 12th-century ruins – are open at certain times and are especially lovely when the snowdrops are in flower. The Shire Hall Museum houses a Georgian courthouse and a lock-up prison, with displays about Walsingham as a place of pilgrimage since 1601. The pump house in the village centre originally had a pinnacle, but this broke during celebrations for victory at Mafeking in 1900. In Great Walsingham the Textile Centre has displays of pots, sculpture and carpets, as well as hand-printed screens.

WHILE YOU'RE THERE The Wells and Walsingham Light Railway has its terminus at the Walsinghams and will take you to the coast. The Thursford Collection at Thursford has displays of mechanical organs, as well as live entertainment, picnic sites and shops. To the south is Pensthorpe Waterfowl Park and Nature Reserve, a magical 200-acre (81ha) site of lakes, woods and meadows.

A Nature Reserve at East Wretham Heath

DISTANCE 2.75 miles (4.4km)	MINIMUM TIME 1hr

ASCENT/GRADIENT Negligible ▲▲▲   LEVEL OF DIFFICULTY ✚✚✚

PATHS Gravel track and waymarked trails across heath

LANDSCAPE Heathland with some sparse pine plantations

SUGGESTED MAP OS Explorer 229 Thetford Forest in The Brecks

START/FINISH Grid reference: TL913885

DOG FRIENDLINESS Dogs are only allowed on the section between Points ❶ and ❺, and must be kept on a short lead between 1 March and 31 July

PARKING Norfolk Wildlife Trust car park off A1075 (open 8am–dusk)

PUBLIC TOILETS None on route

When you arrive at East Wretham Nature Reserve and walk a short distance from the busy A1075, you will hear waterfowl clanking and splashing on Langmere, songbirds chattering in the gorse, the bleat of sheep and the hiss of the wind whispering through the pine trees. It is difficult to imagine that, during World War II, this was a large and bustling military base, with thundering Wellington and Lancaster bombers shattering the peace. The Czech Training Unit were based here, a situation similar to the one depicted in the 2002 film *Dark Blue World*.

MILITARY AIRBASE

The heath was acquired in 1938 by the Norfolk Naturalists' Trust (now the Norfolk Wildlife Trust), because the sandy scrub contained such a wide variety of plants and animals. Among its treasures are some rare spiders and moths, and unusual butterflies such as the small skipper, brown argus, grayling and Essex. However, nature came second to defence in 1939, and the Trust was obliged to relinquish the land to the RAF shortly after. The military remained until 1970, but their concrete airstrips, roads and buildings are slowly being colonised by mosses, lichens and wild flowers such as vipers bugloss, dark mullein and wall pepper, indicating that nature has the upper hand once more.

BRECKLAND NATURE RESERVE

The heath was the first nature reserve ever established in Breckland. It owes its current form to grazing by sheep and rabbits, which prevent it from becoming scrubland again. The first rabbits were introduced to England just after the Norman Conquest, when their fur and meat were a highly prized commodity. They were farmed in warrens and were rare and expensive – a far cry from their status today. Their sharp teeth prevent the area from being over-colonised by bracken, allowing delicate wild flowers to thrive. These include hair grass, thyme-leaved speedwell, heath bedstraw, harebells and early forget-me-not.

In the early 19th century, at the time of the Battle of Waterloo, a belt of Scots pines was planted to shelter the heath from the prevailing winds and to help anchor down the light sandy soil. These days, oaks and birches have joined them, providing a haven for yellowhammers, willow warblers, finches and tree pipits. The old pines have been gnarled and moulded by time and winds, and now form dramatic shapes across the Norfolk skyline.

This special area is important for all sorts of reasons. It provides a unique habitat for a number of rare or unusual birds, animals, plants and insects. It is also one of the few surviving areas of Breckland that has not been encroached by farms or other human development. For more information on the Brecklands and the conservation programmes that are currently in operation, contact the Norfolk Wildlife Trust.

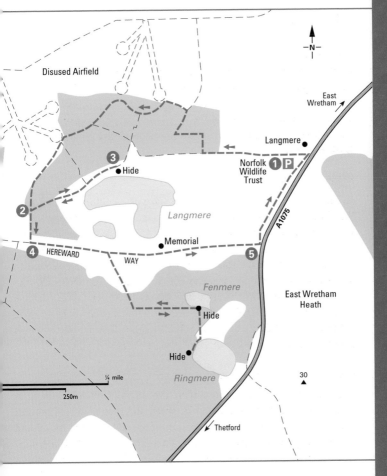

1 From the car park go through the gate and follow the trail marked by green-and-white arrows. This will take you over sandy Breckland heath that is pitted with rabbit warrens, so watch your step. Rabbits can nearly always be seen here. When you reach a kissing gate just after the beginning of a pine plantation, follow the green arrow trail that takes you to the right through the trees. You might notice traces of tarmac underfoot on the route, a relic of the airbase.

2 Follow the green arrows and keep to the paths until you reach a junction of routes. At this point, you could make a short diversion to the left by taking the white trail along the north shore of Langmere, where a narrow path leads down to a bird hide overlooking the lake. The water level in the mere varies from season to season, but the hide is generally a good place to observe waterfowl.

3 Retrace your steps from the hide to the point where the green and white trails converge. Bear left and stay on this path as it crosses a meadow to reach a gate and a fence.

4 Go through the gate and turn left onto old Drove Road. This is part of the Hereward Way and is a wide gravel track with fences on either side. The Norfolk Wildlife Trust opens and closes parts of the reserve depending on the season and weather conditions, but it is usually possible to extend the walk to Fenmere and Ringmere, where there are viewing shelters. If you are able to do this, turn right off the Drove Road and, after reaching Ringmere, return the same way. Look for notices along the road to see if the path is open. The Drove Road will then take you past the memorial to Sydney Herbert Long, who founded the Norfolk Naturalists' Trust in 1926.

5 At the lay-by by the A1075, turn left through a gate and follow the marker posts back to the car park.

WHERE TO EAT AND DRINK There is nowhere to stop for refreshment on the route, since the entire walk is on a nature reserve. However, the Dog and Partridge at nearby East Wretham has good food and a wide range of ales. It has a beer garden at the back, which is a pleasant place to rest after your stroll across the heath.

WHAT TO SEE The stone curlew often visits in the summer. You can identify it by its 'coolee' call and, when it is flying, by the white bands on its wings. Look for crossbills in the pines, feeding with their sharp beaks among the pine cones. They are not native to the area, but will come if the pine crops fail in Scandinavia.

WHILE YOU'RE THERE You can continue walking west along the Drove Road, which is also known as the Hereward Way, to the Devil's Punchbowl, a sinister tree-shrouded pool. The town of Thetford is also worth a visit. It has one of the tallest castle mounds in the country – about 80ft (24m) – dating from before 1086, along with the remains of a once-powerful Cluniac priory.

On Thompson Common

DISTANCE 5.75 miles (9.2km)   MINIMUM TIME 2hrs 30min

ASCENT/GRADIENT 33ft (10m) ▲▲▲   LEVEL OF DIFFICULTY +++

PATHS Wide grassy footpaths to narrow muddy ones, some steps

LANDSCAPE Woodland, heathland and meadow

SUGGESTED MAP OS Explorer 229 Thetford Forest in The Brecks

START/FINISH Grid reference: TL940965

DOG FRIENDLINESS Dogs permitted on old railway line but not in nature reserve

PARKING Great Eastern Pingo Trail car park off A1075

PUBLIC TOILETS None on route

In 1869 trains steamed their way regularly down the 3-mile (4.8km) stretch between Stow Bedon and Great Hockham. The line, known locally as the Crab and Winkle, was particularly busy during World War II, when it was used by servicemen from nearby RAF Watton. However, all rolling stock stopped rolling here in the Beeching cuts of 1965, when the service was declared uneconomical.

In 1971 the county council bought the land, thinking it would make an excellent route for part of the A1075, but plans changed and the road was built elsewhere. The council was left with a narrow strip of land that was not particularly useful, but with great foresight and imagination they decided to develop it as a public footpath. All along the first part of the route you will see reminders of the days when this was busy with trains, with cuttings and embankments and the occasional ruins of a railway employee's cottage shrouded in brambles. The wood and metal bridge across the stream near Thompson Carr has a distinct look of the railway about it, and sturdy sleepers are used to raise the footpath above the marshier segments of the route.

BRECKLAND'S PINGOS

Among the more curious features of the walk are the pingos. These are shallow depressions, often filled with water, that were formed about 20,000 years ago during the last ice age. Bubbles of ice formed underground and expanded, like a large, slippery lens. This lens forced up the soil above it, but years of foul weather washed most of it down the sides again, where it formed a rim around the bottom. When the great glaciers finally retreated north, the underground ice bubbles melted, leaving behind small craters – hollow centres with built-up lips around the edges. Some of these filled with water, forming shallow pools that today teem with wildlife.

Pingos are common in tundra areas like Greenland and Alaska, but they are less obvious in Britain. At one time there were pingos in a wide band across the whole of the Breckland, but many have been lost through ploughing when the fields were cultivated. Fortunately, the ones around Thompson Water have been left alone and today the area boasts the highest concentration of these unusual features in Breckland.

Near Thompson Water you will see signs indicating that the land to your left is a military firing range. The Stanford Training Area, used by up to 80,000 soldiers each year, is also a Site of Special Scientific Interest (SSSI) and parts of it are left to nature.

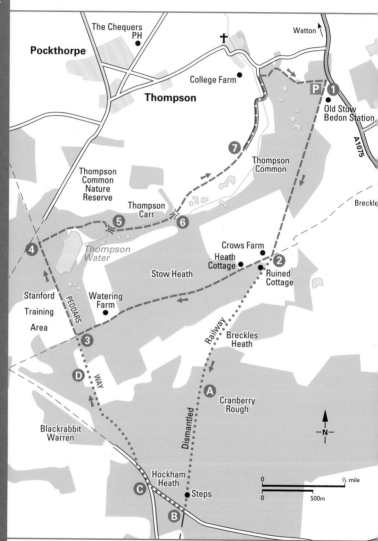

1 From the car park, which is set a short way back from the main road, go through the gate to take the straight path in front of you, marked Great Eastern Pingo Trail and Wayland Walks. Pass the old Stow Bedon station buildings and continue ahead on the disused railway line, part of the Great Eastern railway which gives the walk its name. The path runs through mixed woodland and after a little more than a mile (1.6km) reaches a farm track.

2 Turn right along the track, passing Crows Farm and Heath Cottage on your right, and stay on this forest track as it crosses a couple of woodland rides and passes through the dense mixed woodland of Stow Heath. On reaching Watering Farm, keep straight ahead to a junction.

3 Turn right along the gravelled footpath of the north–south Peddars Way trail. After passing a Norfolk Songline sculpture you will soon see Thompson Water – a shallow artificial lake built in the 1840s – through the trees on your right. On your left note the signs warning that this is an area used by the Ministry of Defence. Once the lake emerges on your right, look out for a sign for the Great Eastern Pingo Trail by a fingerpost that says 'Stow Bedon 4km'.

4 Turn right into the Thompson Common Nature Reserve. Bear left towards a gate and go through to follow the trail around the north end

of the lake, passing a bird hide on the way. Continue past ponds to reach a T-junction with a waymark post semi-hidden behind an oak and a holly bush. Turn right to follow the track through coppiced hazel woodland until crossing a bridge over a sluggish stream. This part of the walk can be muddy, and may necessitate some acrobatics across fallen trees and through sticky black bogs.

5 Turn left after you go over the bridge, and walk next to the stream along a shady path.

6 Cross another bridge, to go through a gate away from the stream and out into the open area of Thompson Common, a meadow kept in good condition by a flock of grazing Shetland sheep. At the end of the meadow go through a gate to follow the path along the side of fields, with several pingos over the hedge to the right. This continues to join a paved lane by a wooden barn.

7 At the lane, continue into the outskirts of the village itself. Pass a number of houses, until you see the Pingo Trail sign to your right, just before a 'Give Way' sign. Follow it through the woodland to arrive back at the car park.

WHERE TO EAT AND DRINK The Chequers at Thompson is an attractive 17th-century thatched pub with original oak beams. It serves home-cooked food at lunch and dinner, and has a garden and children's play area. Dogs are welcome in the garden and public bar.

WHAT TO SEE On the western side of Thompson Water look for the large slate monument for Norfolk Songline Sculptures on the Peddars Way, with its poem commemorating ancient footpaths and ancestors. The monument is modern and its verse is printed sideways on. Thompson village church is away from the main settlement, suggesting a population shift at some point in its history, perhaps due to plague. College Farm stands on the site of a priests' school that was founded in 1349 by the Shardelowe family.

Great Eastern Pingo Trail

DISTANCE 7 miles (11.3km) **MINIMUM TIME** 2hrs 45min

ASCENT/GRADIENT 66ft (20m) ▲▲▲ **LEVEL OF DIFFICULTY** ✚✚✚

SEE MAP AND INFORMATION PANEL FOR WALK 28

The full version of the Pingo Trail is 7 miles (11.3km), and many walkers feel its furthest reaches have the most to offer. If you enjoy silence and solitude, then you may want to complete the circuit.

At Point ❷ keep straight ahead, passing an information board and the stone foundations of the old railway keeper's cottage, dating from 1870, on your right. Cross Breckles Heath to enter the woods and arrive at Cranberry Rough, Point Ⓐ. Once a large glacial lake, this is now a swampy area of woodland where mosquitoes can be a problem in summer. You plunge into a railway cutting and it is easy to imagine the steam engines making their way along it, filling the gully with smoke. Eventually, look out for eight wooden steps, marked with the Pingo Trail sign. Climb the steps, follow the path around a conifer plantation and turn right when you reach a lane at Hockham Heath, Point Ⓑ. Stay on the lane until you see the 'No Through Road' sign at Point Ⓒ. Keep ahead at this sign.

After 200yds (183m) reach a fork. Take the unpaved track on the right, marked as the Peddars Way Circular Walk and National Cycle Network

trail 13. Tall pines grow around you, whispering softly in the wind – which is the only sound you will hear unless the aeroplanes are up and about from the nearby airfield. The ground is covered in ferns and wood chips, making for comfortable walking.

You may be alarmed by the signs on your left, Point Ⓓ, that say it is a military firing range, and that you should keep out. This area was commandeered by the government in 1942 for training troops and is known as the Stanford Training Area. Stanford was the name of its biggest village and about 1,000 people were 'temporarily' evacuated as part of the war effort. The villagers expected to go home in 1945, but they were never allowed to. Occasionally, permission is granted for them to attend family graves, but most of the time the settlements lie forlorn in the middle of bomb-pitted terrain. The training area represents some of the best untouched Breckland heath in Norfolk – a peculiar advantage of sectioning off certain tracts of the countryside for defence purposes.

Look out for the track from Watering Farm on your right-hand side, where you rejoin Walk 28 at Point ❸.

Exploring the Little Ouse from Thetford

DISTANCE 5.25 miles (8.4km)   MINIMUM TIME 2hrs

ASCENT/GRADIENT 33ft (10m) ▲▲▲   LEVEL OF DIFFICULTY ✚✚✚

PATHS Mostly earth tracks, some concrete footpaths and meadows

LANDSCAPE Riverside water-meadows and forest

SUGGESTED MAP OS Explorer 229 Thetford Forest in The Brecks

START/FINISH Grid reference: TL868830

DOG FRIENDLINESS Lead required in town

PARKING Town car park (free) off Bridge Street beside river

PUBLIC TOILETS At car park

On 1 September, 1107, an old warrior friend of William the Conqueror called Roger Bigod stooped to lay the foundation stone of what he hoped would be a great priory church – also hoping that the Cluniac monks who would live there would pray for his immortal soul. He had left it not a moment too long, for he died a week later. He wanted to be buried at Thetford, but was not in a position to argue when the Bishop of Norwich took his body off to his own cathedral for subsequent burial.

A CLUNIAC HERITAGE

Today the silent ruins that stand beside the peaceful River Ouse belie the fact that this was once a powerful and wealthy community. Besides the large church, there was a huge cloister, a warming house with a sleeping room above, an infirmary, a dining room and a number of kitchens and parlours. The Cluniac monks lived a comfortable life, compared to many others.

In the 13th century, a very ill local craftsman prayed to the Virgin Mary to make him well; she appeared to him in dreams and told him to build a Lady Chapel. When the prior ignored the craftsman's pleas, the Virgin is said to have gone to a local woman instead, paralysing her arm when she did not inform the prior of the message immediately. The chapel was built and, while an old statue of the Virgin was being cleaned to be its centrepiece, a hole was found in its head. Inside the hole were relics, which were said to have fabulous healing powers. For many years, the sick and desperate paid the priory handsomely to be allowed near the statue.

THE RIGHTS OF MAN

One of Thetford's most famous sons is Thomas Paine, whose statue can be seen in King Street holding a copy of his book, *The Rights of Man*.

Born in Thetford in 1737, the son of a corset maker, Paine attended Thetford Grammar School before becoming an apprentice to his father. He went to sea aged 19 and, after trying his hand as a tax officer, emigrated to the US in 1774. It was here that he turned to journalism and became a strong supporter of American independence from Great Britain. Returning to Europe he wrote *The Rights of Man*. Outlawed for his anti-monarchist views, Paine fled to revolutionary France where he was subsequently imprisoned for pleading clemency in the execution of Louis XVI. He died in New York in 1809, his funeral attended by just a handful of mourners, reflecting his humanist views.

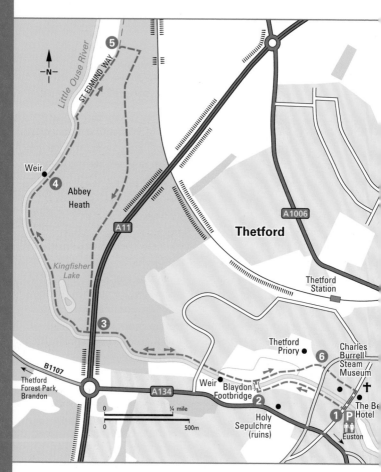

❶ Head for the splendid red, gold and green Town Bridge (built in 1829). Cross the road and go down the peaceful river path opposite with the river on your right. Passing underneath a road bridge, you will be able to make out the ruins of

Thetford Priory to the right across the river. When you reach the Blaydon Footbridge (built in 1970 and named after a local dignitary), take a few minutes to head to the main road and turn left. Here you will find the ruins of the little medieval Church of the

Holy Sepulchre, and opposite, the site of Red Castle, Thetford's second fort, raised in the 12th century.

2 Return to the footbridge and cross over it, then turn left along the river bank to stroll through water-meadows and past a weir. When the path bears right to meet a road, keep straight ahead under a bridge. You are now on the Little Ouse Path to Brandon, which is rich with the scent of meadowsweet in springtime.

3 Continue beneath the roaring bypass, and past the still, brown Kingfisher Lake where local folk sit to fish. You leave the sounds of the town behind you as you reach Abbey Heath Weir. When the path bends, keep to the river track, which is littered with sandy molehills.

4 When the path veers to the right, gently uphill away from the river, continue along this through dense Forestry Commission woodland, ignoring the broad forestry track off to the right.

5 Emerging from the woods, turn right up a grassy track, which leads slightly uphill towards a railway bridge. When you reach a T-junction just before the railway bridge, turn right along the dirt road used by Forestry Commission vehicles. Stay on this track as the sound of the bypass traffic grows increasingly loud to your left. The track ends at the main road, but a path to your right leads you through a gate and down an incline, where you will find yourself at the underpass again. Retrace your steps along the river to Blaydon Footbridge, but do not cross it. Continue across the grass straight ahead past willows to reach an electricity station.

6 The remains of Thetford Priory (free) are off to the left. After visiting the remains return to the electricity station and go under the subway to Minstergate. Walk past the Charles Burrell Steam Museum until you reach The Bell Hotel. Turn right to the bridge. The car park is now on your left.

WHERE TO EAT AND DRINK There are several places to eat in Thetford near the end of the walk. The Bell Hotel has a restaurant and also serves bar meals, with families welcome. Steel River Blues is a floating restaurant moored by the Town Bridge, serving pasta, steaks and daytime snacks.

WHAT TO SEE Stroll by the River Ouse to see the waterfowl – but the geese and swans can be aggressive when they have young to protect, so prepare to give them a wide berth. While in the town, look for the old pump room on Spring Walk (built in 1818), and the early Tudor timber-framed Ancient House, now the Museum of Thetford Life. Outside the King's House is a statue commemorating Thomas Paine, revolutionary author of *The Rights of Man*.

WHILE YOU'RE THERE Visit nearby Thetford Forest for outdoor activities including cycling and an adventurous rope course. Three miles (4.8km) southeast is the pretty village of Euston. Splendid 18th-century Euston Hall (limited summer opening) is the country seat of the Dukes of Grafton. It's notable for its fine collection of pictures by Stubbs, Lely and Van Dyck.

Overleaf: Breckland pines at daybreak, Thetford (Walk 30)

Around Great Cressingham

DISTANCE 5.75 miles (9.2km)	MINIMUM TIME 2hrs 30min

ASCENT/GRADIENT 164ft (50m) ▲▲▲   LEVEL OF DIFFICULTY ✦✦✦

PATHS Paved country lanes

LANDSCAPE Gently undulating farmland

SUGGESTED MAP OS Explorer 236 King's Lynn, Downham Market & Swaffham

START/FINISH Grid reference: TF845018

DOG FRIENDLINESS Dogs can run free, but watch for traffic

PARKING Car park opposite The Olde Windmill Inn, Great Cressingham

PUBLIC TOILETS None on route

Most of us have seen pheasants strutting proudly along the side of the road or standing nobly in recently ploughed fields looking for seeds and grubs. Their metallic coughing calls emanating from woodlands and culverts is also a familiar country sound. You may well encounter them around Cressingham, which is noted for its game shoots. However, pheasants have not always been so numerous, and today's large numbers are influenced by the release of captive birds into the countryside for sport.

Pheasants are handsome birds. The males are chestnut-bronze, gorgeously marked with cream and black and an iridescent green-purple sheen. Their featherless faces are scarlet and they have bottle-green heads. Females are less brilliant, and are quiet and sandy-buff coloured. Pheasants have long been considered a delicacy for the table, and at medieval banquets roasted birds were often presented 'redressed' in their original feathers.

A PLACE ON THE ABBOT'S TABLE

Pheasants were known in England as early as AD 1050, when they were mentioned in documents relating to royal feasts. The first reference to them in this country as birds for hunting occurred about 1100, when the Abbot of Amesbury applied for permission to hunt them for his own table. New species were introduced in the 18th and 19th centuries, and comprised mostly ring-necked varieties from central Asia, Japan and China. The Mongolian pheasant was introduced into England as recently as 1900, and immediately started to breed with the species already here.

The word pheasant comes from the Greek *phasianos*, which means 'native of Phasis'. This has its origins in the story of Jason and the Argonauts. When they went to Colchis on the edge of the Black Sea, they came back with more than a mere Golden Fleece: they were said to have returned with pheasants. There may be some truth to this story. Pheasants may well have originated in this region and then been exported by people who saw their potential as food. They were certainly raised in Greece during the life of Pericles (c.495–429 BC), because he mentioned them in his writing, and they appear in the records of the Romans, who considered them a great delicacy. In the 16th and 17th centuries, pheasant hunting became so popular in Europe that laws were passed to protect them.

Pheasants take to the wild readily. The ring-necked species, which are most common here, prefer open woodland, meadows and thickets.

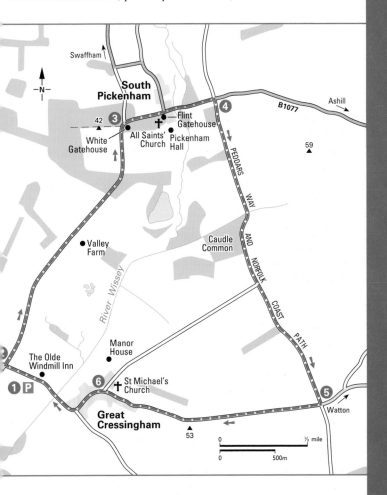

❶ Park opposite The Olde Windmill Inn in Great Cressingham. It takes its name from an old corn mill that once operated near by. Turn left along a peaceful country lane. The grassy verges and hawthorn hedges here are a joy in spring, with nesting thrushes, wrens, blackbirds and robins. After about 350yds (320m) you will reach a crossroads.

2 Turn right along the lane marked to South Pickenham, which runs parallel to the River Wissey. Some of the trees on this lane – oaks, chestnuts and beeches – were planted in the 19th century. After several large open arable fields and then Valley Farm and vineyard to the right, the lane passes through a shady wood of beech and oak where pheasants nest. After the woods look for the meadow with mature trees on your right. Modern agricultural methods mean that trees are seldom tolerated in the middle of fields these days, but this is part of the South Pickenham estate that was carefully landscaped centuries ago with mature trees and grazing meadows.

3 Turn right when you get to the junction by the white gatehouse, and join the Peddars Way bridle route towards Ashill. This is another wooded lane, with the sturdy walls of the Pickenham Hall estate to the right. Before long, you will see the distinctive round tower of South Pickenham's All Saints' Church. Go straight on at the next junction towards Ashill. Pickenham Hall can be

seen off to the right beyond the flint gatehouse. This lane can be plagued by fast-driving cars, so you need to be vigilant and walk with care. Cross the brick bridge over the River Wissey and continue to the next junction.

4 Turn right along a narrow lane, which is part of the long distance National Trail, the Peddars Way and Norfolk Coast Path, and continue along it for a little less than 2 miles (3.2km), until you reach a crossroads at a main road.

5 Turn right again and continue until you get to Great Cressingham. St Michael's Church, which you will pass, has flint walls and large Gothic windows. Note the carvings above the tower door – each shield is crowned with the letter 'M', standing for St Michael. If you go inside, look for the 15th-century stained glass and brasses.

6 Leave the church and follow the main road as it bears left into the village. Turn right at the T-junction back to the car park.

WHERE TO EAT AND DRINK The Olde Windmill Inn offers a varied menu, including one for children, and there is a wide selection of beers. Dogs are allowed inside if they are well behaved. The pub has a 14th-century fireplace and an intriguing collection of Victorian photographs, including one of the corn mill after which the pub was named.

WHAT TO SEE Great Cressingham Manor House was once known as Great Cressingham Priory, although there was never a religious house here. It dates from the 1540s. Pickenham Hall was built for the banker G W Taylor in 1902 by the prominent Arts and Crafts architect Robert Weir Schultz. Although it is not open to visitors, you will be able to sneak a glimpse of it through the trees as you walk around its walled grounds.

WHILE YOU'RE THERE Thetford Forest, to the west, offers a selection of marked walking and cycling trails of different lengths and difficulties. The little town of Watton, to the east, is a thriving community with small shops and a 12th-century church. It was granted permission to hold a market by King John in the 13th century, and maintains the tradition every Wednesday. Ecotech, at Swaffham, is also worth a visit (see Walk 35).

Weeting Castle to Grimes Graves

DISTANCE 7.5 miles (12.1km)   MINIMUM TIME 3hrs

ASCENT/GRADIENT 148ft (45m) ▲▲▲   LEVEL OF DIFFICULTY +++

PATHS Farm and forest tracks, some roads

LANDSCAPE Farmland and commercial forest

SUGGESTED MAP OS Explorer 229 Thetford Forest in The Brecks

START/FINISH Grid reference: TL776891

DOG FRIENDLINESS Dogs must be kept on lead in forest and near farms

PARKING Lay-by at Weeting Castle, next to church

PUBLIC TOILETS Temporary toilets at Grimes Graves

NOTES This walk can only be done between April and early November, when Grimes Graves (English Heritage) is open. At other times, the entrance gate is locked and access is not permitted

All that remains of Weeting Castle are a few teetering, rugged grey stone walls standing amid mature trees and long grass. However, in the 12th century this was a comfortable and relatively secure house. It comprised two floors: the lower one was used for storage and the upper one provided the main accommodation. The order to build it was probably given by William de Warenne, the Earl of Surrey, a friend of William the Conqueror. The man who did all the building work was Hugh de Plais, de Warenne's tenant at Weeting.

Weeting Castle was never intended to be a defensive structure, like de Warenne's sturdy motte and bailey at nearby Castle Acre, but was a manor house surrounded by a wet moat. While this would not have hindered a serious attack, it was considered sufficient to repel the casual robber. The moat was rectangular and still exists, albeit in a rather more shallow form.

GRIMES GRAVES

At the other end of the walk lie the mysterious humps and bumps in the grass that represent Europe's largest prehistoric flint mine. These were dug by folk in the Stone Age some 4,000 years ago, and were a large and prosperous enterprise. High-quality Grimes Graves flint has been identified for miles around, suggesting that it was prized for making sharp tools (like axe- and arrowheads) and that it was in demand over much of southern England.

For many years, no one could work out how the peculiar pitted surface of this area had been formed. Various explanations emerged. Some proposed that the pits were actually graves, while the Saxons believed they were devil's holes, perhaps made by the pagan god Grim – hence the name Grimes Graves. It was not until 1870 that they were properly excavated, and then it was discovered that the 400 or so circular depressions are actually filled-in mine shafts. The rock in the shafts is very dense, and it was hacked out by men using picks made from the antlers of red deer. Their objective was to locate nodes of hard, black flint with no flaws. This was roughly knapped on a site near by, then sent off to be traded.

Visit early in the morning, when mist swirls over the hollows and only birds break the silence, and you will understand very well how legends of pagan sacrifices and sculpting by the devil originated.

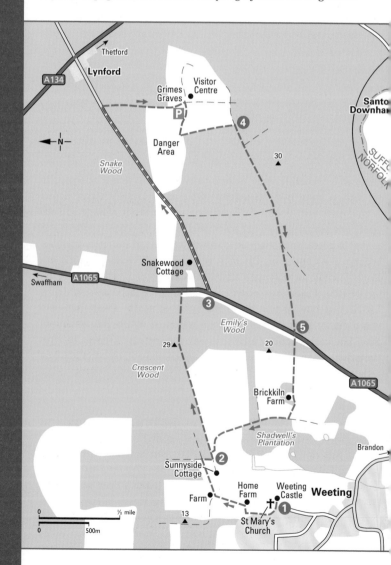

1 Park in the sandy lay-by at the sign for Weeting Castle. Go through a kissing gate and walk across the meadow to look at the remains of this fortified manor house, then follow the farm track past St Mary's Church, with its round tower. Go through Home Farm, past farm buildings to the right, and then follow the track as it bends left past pig units in a field to the left. After walking past the pig enclosures, turn right by an isolated farmhouse and head towards the trees, turning right again on reaching a T-junction.

2 At the junction by Sunnyside Cottage, take the left-hand turn, following the track with woodland on the left and a huge open field on the right. After about 0.6 miles (965m) you pass through woodland on both sides before finally reaching the A1065 after about a mile (1.6km). Turn right and walk for about 350yds (320m) along the verge.

3 Cross the A1065 and then follow the paved lane signposted to Grimes Graves and West Tofts. Stay on this road past Snakewood Cottage on the left and a bridleway on the right, until you see a sign on your right for Grimes Graves after about 1.25 miles (2km). Pass through the gate and walk down the approach road to enter the site. You will need to pay an entrance fee, even to walk here. From the car

park, follow the path to your right leading across the heath to an area of tall trees beside a Ministry of Defence firing area. Cross the stile over the perimeter fence, then turn left to walk along the outside of the fence to the corner of the site.

4 Turn right at a junction of paths. After 200yds (183m) you will see a sunken water butt with a corrugated-iron roof, looking like a house that has half-disappeared into the ground. Go straight across this junction and walk along the broad gravel track to the A1065 again. Despite the proximity of the main road, you are in the depths of prime forest here.

5 Cross the A1065 and take the sandy track directly opposite. After a short walk, the woods give way to farmland again as the oak-lined track continues through fields. Pass Brickkiln Farm and ignore the track going off to the right. When you reach the end of the field, turn right and walk along the side of Shadwell's Plantation (recalling the Weeting poet Thomas Shadwell, who died in 1691). Keep straight ahead when the track divides at the end of the plantation, and stay on this track until it rejoins the outward path by Sunnyside Cottage. Retrace your steps past the pig farm back to the car park.

WHERE TO EAT AND DRINK There is nowhere to eat on this route, but the English Heritage shop at Grimes Graves sells chocolate and snacks. For something more substantial, The Saxon, on the main road through the village of Weeting, serves generous portions of home-cooked food and Brandon ales.

WHAT TO SEE Today most of the shafts at Grimes Graves are blocked up, but English Heritage has excavated one, and visitors can don hard hats and climb down into its depths. The ladder descends about 30ft (9m) to a bulb-like hollow, where several short tunnels have been dug off to the sides.

WHILE YOU'RE THERE Visit historic Thetford (see Walk 30) with its 12th-century Cluniac priory and its huge 11th-century castle mound.

Overleaf: Boats at Burnham Overy Staithe (Walk 33)

On Nelson's Trail at Burnham Overy

DISTANCE 4 miles (6.4km)	MINIMUM TIME 2hrs

ASCENT/GRADIENT 49ft (15m) ▲▲▲   LEVEL OF DIFFICULTY ✤✤✤

PATHS Waymarked paths and some paved lanes

LANDSCAPE Wild salt marshes and mudflats, fields and meadows

SUGGESTED MAP AA Walker's Map 21 North Norfolk Coast

START/FINISH Grid reference: TF844442

DOG FRIENDLINESS On lead in nature reserves and under strict control on farmland

PARKING On-street parking on main road in Burnham Overy Staithe, or off-road at the harbour

PUBLIC TOILETS None on route

In 1758 Edmund Nelson, rector of Burnham Thorpe, and his wife Catherine had the fifth of their 11 children and named him Horatio. The rectory where Horatio Nelson spent the first years of his life was demolished in 1802 and a new one built. However, when you visit Burnham Thorpe you will see a plaque set in a wall where the old rectory once stood.

NELSON'S LIFE

Nelson was just 12 when he entered the Royal Navy. He quickly gained experience, travelling as far afield as the Caribbean and the Arctic by the time he was 16. He went to India, but was sent home after contracting malaria. Throughout his travels he was plagued by seasickness – a fact in which many novice seamen find comfort. Nelson became a captain at the age of 20 and spent some years in the West Indies, where he enforced British law a little too vigorously for the Admiralty, who refused to give him another command until war broke out with France in 1792. During this frustrating time, Nelson lived in Burnham Thorpe with his wife Frances (Fanny). Once back in service he was sent to the Mediterranean, but was blinded in his right eye by splinters from a parapet struck by enemy fire. Undaunted, he returned to duty the following day.

When he left the Mediterranean in 1797, Nelson's small fleet encountered a much larger French one. Due largely to his unusual tactics, the British inflicted an embarrassing defeat on the French, leading to a knighthood for Nelson. He lost his arm in the Canary Islands when trying to capture Spanish treasure and was wounded yet again in the Battle of the Nile – from which he emerged victorious. He was then nursed by Emma, Lady Hamilton, who later become his lover. Elevation to the peerage as Baron Nelson of the Nile followed.

His brazen affair with Lady Hamilton (who became pregnant with their daughter Horatia) led to an estrangement from his wife, and lack of money forced him to apply for active service again. In 1805 he was fatally wounded at the Battle of Trafalgar.

Look out for the bust of Nelson above his father's tomb in All Saints' Church, along with flags from his battles. The Lord Nelson pub at Burnham Thorpe has a collection of memorabilia.

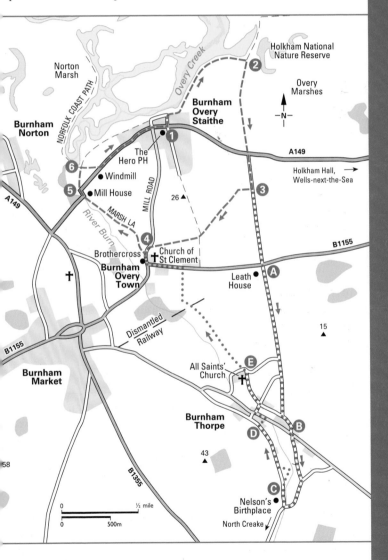

1 From The Hero pub, turn right, then immediately left down East Harbour Way until you reach Overy

Creek. Turn right next to the black-painted house, go through a gate and then bear left along the waterfront.

The bank you are on was raised to protect the adjacent land from sudden incursions by the sea and is part of the long distance Norfolk Coast Path National Trail.

2 Where the path along the embankment goes 90 degrees left, turn right, through the gate, into a marshy meadow of long grass. This area is a Natural England reserve (part of Holkham National Nature Reserve) and the sand dunes, salt marshes and mudflats are home to a wide variety of birds and plants, including plovers and sea asters. Go through a second gate, cross a stile, then continue along the track until you reach the A149. Cross to the lane opposite, and follow this until you have passed two fields on your right.

3 Go through the gap at the entrance to the third field, which is marked as a footpath. Keep to the right of the hedge until you reach a waymarker pointing left, across the middle of the field. Keep going in a straight line, through gaps in hedges, following the circular markers with yellow arrows until you reach a dirt lane. Cross this and go down the track opposite, with hedges on

either side, towards the Norman tower of Burnham Overy's Church of St Clement, topped by a 17th-century bell turret.

4 Turn left at the end of the track onto Mill Road, then take the grass track to the right, called Marsh Lane. Go through the gate and into a field, so that the River Burn is off to your left, with the round Saxon tower of Burnham Norton in the distance to your left and Burnham Overy windmill straight ahead. Go through the gate by Mill House, complete with mill pond and mill race (1820).

5 Cross the A149, with the pond on your left, then take the public footpath into the next field. Cross the stile and keep the hedge to your right. In the distance you will see the sails of Burnham Overy windmill, which is privately owned and not usually open to the public.

6 Cross a stile and turn right onto the Norfolk Coast Path, then continue to the A149. Turn left and follow the path beside the road to East Harbour Way on the left and The Hero pub on the right.

WHERE TO EAT AND DRINK Start or finish your walk with an excellent meal at The Hero Bar and Restaurant, which offers home-made dishes using locally-sourced produce. There is a patio area where well-behaved dogs are welcome.

WHAT TO SEE In the marshes, particularly the sections that are nature reserves, look for sea aster and samphire. In the summer months, you will also see the purple bloom of sea lavender. Besides wading birds that inhabit the salt marshes and mudflats all year, you will also see noisy brent geese, with their characteristic black heads and white rumps, in the winter.

WHILE YOU'RE THERE You can explore the seven Burnhams – Market, Overy, Overy Staithe, Overy Town, Norton, Deepdale and Thorpe. Burnham Norton's church has a Saxon round tower, while Burnham Market has a handsome green, fringed by elegant 18th-century houses. Along the coast to the east is Holkham Hall with its Bygones Museum, while nearby Wells-next-the-Sea (which isn't really) is famous for its whelks and sprats.

From Burnham Overy to Burnham Thorpe

DISTANCE 7.5 miles (12.1km)   MINIMUM TIME 2hrs 30min

ASCENT/GRADIENT 82ft (25m) ▲▲▲   LEVEL OF DIFFICULTY +++

SEE MAP AND INFORMATION PANEL FOR WALK 33

The River Burn is a placid stream that meanders slowly through its pretty little valley of attractive meadows, dotted with sheep in the summer. Monks and friars obviously thought this was a good place to live, because two religious orders founded priories here in the past.

The tranquillity of the valley was rudely shattered in 1953 and again in 1978, when north winds and high spring tides caused the sea defences to fail and water came rushing in. The result was devastating, with the river bursting its banks and flooding the homes and farms.

Begin the extension at Point ❸: instead of going across the field, continue down the lane towards Burnham Thorpe. Large fields stretch away on either side. When you reach the crossroads, with Leath House to your right, Point ❹, continue past the houses into a shady lane, with orchards to the left and right, shielded from the bitter sea winds by hedges.

Keep to the left at the first junction as you arrive in Burnham Thorpe, and take the road towards The Creakes at the second junction, Point ❸. Here are the best views of the valley of the River Burn. The road loops round to the right – go right at the T-junction and follow the sign to Nelson's birthplace, Point ❻, marked by a plaque on the wall. This was given to the village by one of his officers.

Take the footpath opposite the parsonage to follow the river for a while, then rejoin the lane. On reaching Burnham Thorpe, go right on Garners Row, Point ❼. At the end of the street go left to the Nelson sign, then right onto Lowes Lane, to the lane that leads to All Saints' Church.

The rood in the chancel arch is made up of timbers from Nelson's flagship at Trafalgar, HMS *Victory*. Where the lane bends left around the church, go through a kissing gate onto a footpath, Point ❸, over a stile then across a meadow, with the river to your left.

The path goes through another kissing gate, then crosses an old railway embankment, jinking left before heading north along a field-edge. Eventually, the path reaches a lane. Turn left and walk into Burnham Overy Town, past the broken Brothercross, where villagers once traded their wares. Turn right when you reach the junction, and then rejoin the main route at Point ❹.

A Circuit from Swaffham

DISTANCE 5.25 miles (8.4km)	MINIMUM TIME 2hrs 15min

ASCENT/GRADIENT 131ft (40m) ▲▲▲   LEVEL OF DIFFICULTY +++

PATHS Roads, paved lanes and public footpaths

LANDSCAPE Country town and its surrounding farmland

SUGGESTED MAP OS Explorer 236 King's Lynn, Downham Market & Swaffham

START/FINISH Grid reference: TF819089

DOG FRIENDLINESS Lead required in town, and under strict control on the lanes

PARKING Car park in centre of Swaffham, by Market Cross

PUBLIC TOILETS None on route

The walk begins in the centre of Swaffham, near the Market Cross. Once called the Butter Cross, this Palladian-style structure is topped by a little figure of the goddess Ceres, holding a sheaf. It was given to the town by Lord Orford in 1783. Swaffham owes much of its present-day elegance to late 18th-century and Regency times, when it was a centre for well-connected people to attend balls, soirées and concerts.

REGENCY SWAFFHAM

One of the places they met was the handsome Assembly Rooms, now a school, built between 1776 and 1778. There was also a theatre, which entertained such august personages as Horatio, Lord Nelson and his family (and his mistress, too, according to the records). People gathered in Swaffham for 'the season', and so many clergymen ranked among their numbers that the Bishop of Norwich was reported as being concerned that they were neglecting their parishioners.

One of the most prestigious events in the days of the Regency was the annual hare coursing hosted by the Swaffham Club. This was established by Lord Orford, a nephew of the writer Horace Walpole, in 1786. He had a fine hound called Czarina, who regularly chased hares across the heaths surrounding Swaffham. She is thought to be the ancestor of every pure greyhound alive today. When she was completing her 47th – and final – race, Orford became so excited that he fell off his horse and died.

THE SWAFFHAM PEDLAR

The town is well known for the legend of the so-called Swaffham Pedlar, a local man called John Chapman who had gone to London and met a stranger on London Bridge. The stranger told him about a dream in which he had gone to garden (the one he had described was the pedlar's own) and excavated a huge treasure trove. The pedlar set off home with great haste, discovered the treasure and donated his money to the town's church. Legend has it that the fabulous Tudor windows of the north aisle of the Church of St Peter and St Paul were paid for by Chapman. The Swaffham Pedlar also appears in the hand-carved Swaffham town sign.

Another famous local was Howard Carter, the eminent 20th-century Egyptologist who discovered Tutankhamun's tomb in the Valley of the Kings and is rumoured to have died as the result of the boy-king's curse. An exhibition of Carter's work in Egypt can be seen in the town museum, which also serves as the tourist information centre.

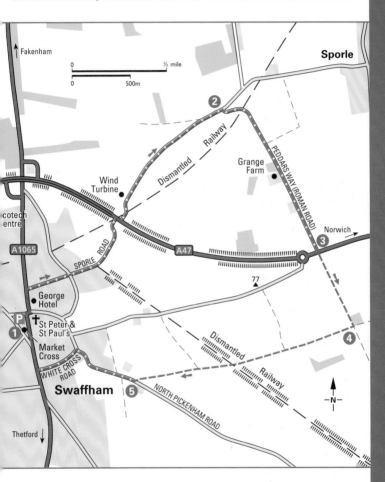

❶ Walk across the road to the Red Lion pub on the east side of the square, and head north with the Market Cross behind you. Almost immediately you pass the entrance to the parish Church of St Peter and St Paul's, which dates mostly from the 15th century and whose distinctive

spire can be seen for miles around. After exploring the church, continue to head north and cross the road at a busy junction with traffic lights, passing the George Hotel. Walk on the pavement along Station Road until you see Sporle Road on your right. Turn right and stay on this road as it passes through a residential area, before keeping straight ahead at a crossroads and passing through a cutting in a disused railway. The road bends left and heads into the countryside, with the sails of a giant wind turbine turning up ahead. When you reach the A47, cross it (very carefully) and aim for the lane opposite and slightly to the right, passing beneath the wind turbine on your left. After about 0.5 miles (800m) you reach a sign on your right saying 'Peddars Way – Restricted Byway Pickenham 3km'.

2 Follow the lane over a bridge over a disused railway line and past Grange Farm, to eventually reach the A47 once more.

3 Cross the busy road and head for the path for cyclists and walkers only. Keep straight ahead on an old Roman road, now a shady path, passing a Norfolk Songlines Sculpture on your left, to reach a crossroads.

4 Turn right here and head back in the direction of Swaffham. The path crosses the dismantled railway and, after about a mile (1.6km) of peaceful traffic-free walking, comes out on the North Pickenham Road. In this vast open landscape, it is easy to appreciate the power of the wind. Two giant wind turbines dominate the views to your right, and the eight turbines of the wind farm at North Pickenham are visible across the fields to your left.

5 Turn right along the lane to head back into town. Climb to a junction and then turn left along White Cross Road. At the end of this road, turn right along London Street to return to the town centre and car park.

WHERE TO EAT AND DRINK There are several good choices in Swaffham for snacks and meals, including the Red Lion on Market Cross and the George Hotel near the start of the walk. If you get hungry halfway round, there is a drive-through McDonald's where the Peddars Way crosses the A47.

WHAT TO SEE There is an informative local museum above the town hall, where you will be entertained by the story of John Chapman and his buried treasure. A lively market takes place each Saturday, along with an auction. In the Church of St Peter and St Paul's don't miss the superb double hammerbeam roof in the nave, and the chancel.

WHILE YOU'RE THERE Swaffham's Ecotech is a scientific and environmental discovery centre that informs visitors about issues relating to climate change, pollution and alternative power sources. The centrepiece is the Ecotricity Wind Turbine, which, at approximately 215ft (65m), dominates the country for miles. Climb the 300 steps to the top for breathtaking views.

Through Thetford Forest to Lynford

DISTANCE 4.5 miles (7.2km)   MINIMUM TIME 2hrs

ASCENT/GRADIENT 66ft (20m) ▲▲▲   LEVEL OF DIFFICULTY ✚✚✚

PATHS Wide grassy trackways and small paths

LANDSCAPE Coniferous and mixed deciduous forest

SUGGESTED MAP OS Explorer 229 Thetford Forest in The Brecks

START/FINISH Grid reference: TL814917

DOG FRIENDLINESS On lead, and keep away from children's play areas; no dogs (except guide dogs) allowed in arboretum

PARKING Lynford Stag picnic site off A134

PUBLIC TOILETS Close to start

By 1916, with the horrors of World War I in full swing, the British government realised that it could no longer rely on timber imports to supplement Britain's own wood production and sustain industrial output. The huge demands placed on woodland resources by the onset of trench warfare and the spiralling need for colliery pit props brought the realisation that it would have to establish a group responsible for planting strategic timber reserves, as well as chopping them down again. The solution was the Forestry Commission, established immediately after the war in 1919. It began by buying up large tracts of land that were suitable for growing trees. One of the first areas it obtained was the sandy heathland around the ancient priory town of Thetford, because this was an ideal habitat for many species of fast-growing conifers.

By 1935 the new Thetford Forest had reached the boundaries on today's maps. It covers an area of 50,000 acres (20,250ha), and is the largest lowland pine forest in the country. Originally it was dominated by Scots pine, but this was changed to Corsican pine, which allows some 220,000 tons (224,000 tonnes) of timber to be cut every year. The amount taken is carefully controlled, so that the timber industry is sustainable – it never takes more than it plants.

FOREST WILDLIFE

The forest is home to numerous rare animals, birds and plants, including red squirrels, and people travel from miles around to enjoy the peace of the great forest trackways. Lucky visitors who walk quietly may spot one of the park's four species of resident deer: fallow, roe, red and muntjac. It is also home to a large number of bats, including the pipistrelle and the barbastelle. A bat hibernaculum has been built, to give them somewhere to spend the daylight hours.

UNUSUAL TARGET

Lynford Stag is named for the life-sized metal deer that stands unobtrusively among the car parks and picnic benches. This was discovered by workers clearing the area for planting trees, and must have given them quite a surprise when they stumbled across it. In fact, it was made for Sir Richard Sutton, a keen hunter who owned nearby Lynford Hall, and who used it for target practice. Lynford Hall is a Grade II-listed mock-Jacobean mansion standing amid imposing gardens overlooking a series of artificial lakes. The building of 1857 stands on the site of an earlier hall dating from the 1720s.

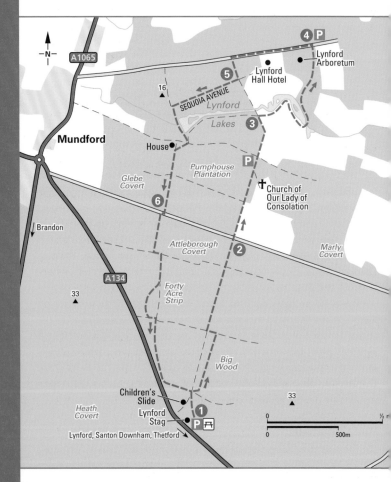

1 From the car park follow the grassy path that runs between the metal stag and the notice board,

parallel to the edge of the trees. When you arrive level with a large children's slide in the form of a stag to the left, turn right and follow the blue marker posts into the trees. Jig slightly to the right and follow the markers heading north. Emerging from the trees turn left along a grassy track then, after passing a bench, turn right at a crossroads of tracks, leaving the blue trail to walk between conifer plantations. Eventually, after crossing another forest track, you reach a paved road.

2 Cross the road and continue ahead on what was once part of the driveway leading to Lynford Hall. Go across a junction of tracks and continue ahead along a gravel path, next to a meadow on the right, picking up the next set of blue and green trails. The Church of Our Lady of Consolation is hidden behind the trees to your right. It was designed by Pugin in the 1870s for the Catholic owner of the hall, but the next owner, a Protestant, planted trees to shield it from view. Shortly, reach a stone bridge and a sign for Lynford Hall Hotel.

3 Turn right and follow the gravel path along the shore of Lynford Lakes, with views across the water to Lynford Hall. Turn left across a bridge to enter Lynford Arboretum, and follow the path through the arboretum until you reach a road.

4 Turn left along the road, passing Lynford Hall Hotel on your left. After you have walked past the building, turn left through the main entrance gates of the hotel and walk up the drive.

5 When you see a sculpture of two bulls fighting, turn right onto a wide grassy sward called Sequoia Avenue. Walk almost to the end of it, then follow the blue markers to the left into the wood. After a few paces you come to the lake. The blue trail bears to the left at the end of the lake, but our walk continues straight ahead on the bridleway. Turn right where the path meets a T-junction then, ignoring another footpath to the right past a house, keep left. Turn left at the driveway to the house to continue along the bridleway.

6 Reach a paved lane and turn right for a few yards before turning left along another track. Continue straight on, through tall conifers. Turn left at the end of the track, then almost immediately right, where you will pick up the blue trail markers again. Follow these to return to the car park.

WHERE TO EAT AND DRINK Lynford Hall Hotel is a perfect place to take a break, as it lies at the halfway point. It offers bar meals and morning and afternoon teas and coffees. The Lynford Stag picnic site has picnic tables and a huge wooden 'play' stag for children. There are ice cream vans here in the summer.

WHAT TO SEE The red squirrel, once a common sight in our woodlands but now sadly depleted, can be found in the forest. Besides deer, you may also see foxes, hares and badgers. Around Lynford Lakes and its drains keep an eye out for frogs, toads and newts.

WHILE YOU'RE THERE Visit the High Lodge Forest Centre at Santon Downham. Attractions include cycle hire and the giant Squirrels' Maze. There are also children's activity days, a shop and cafe, an outdoor theatre and concerts.

Overleaf: The tranquil ruins of Castle Acre Priory (Walk 37)

Around Castle Acre

DISTANCE 6.5 miles (10.4km)   MINIMUM TIME 2hrs 45min

ASCENT/GRADIENT 230ft (70m) ▲▲▲   LEVEL OF DIFFICULTY +++

PATHS Footpaths, trackways and some tiny country lanes; can be very muddy, nettles, some steps

LANDSCAPE Wooded river valley, open fields

SUGGESTED MAP AA Leisure Map 6 North West Norfolk

START/FINISH Grid reference: TF817151

DOG FRIENDLINESS Can run free, but should be on lead on farmland

PARKING On road by village green, Castle Acre

PUBLIC TOILETS Priory Road, near entrance to Castle Acre Priory

Castle Acre was founded as a daughter Cluniac priory to that at Lewes, in Sussex, and was richly endowed. Trouble erupted as Cluny sought to retain control, but the Norfolk clerics resisted. Things came to a head in 1283, when Prior William discovered that he had been replaced by Benedict of Cluny. William fortified Castle Acre Priory to keep the detested Benedict out. It's easy to imagine poor Benedict standing outside while you explore these remains.

EXPLOITING AN ASSET

Castle Acre Priory was the proud owner of the severed arm of St Philip, which generated a constant stream of generous pilgrims during medieval times. Folk came from near and far to pay homage to the relic, and to ask for boons and cures, and most left a gift of some kind behind. This made the priory wealthy, along with an Indulgence granted by Pope Boniface IX in 1401, which saw even more penitents arriving at its doors. But interest in relics and pilgrimages waned and, by 1533, the revenue from visitors was down to a mere ten shillings per year. Few ripples were caused when the last prior signed away his monastery to Henry VIII.

During its heyday, Castle Acre Priory was one of the finest monasteries in East Anglia, and even today, when most of it comprises crumbling ruins and the foundations of walls in the grass, it is impressive. The site was enormous and was basically a self-contained village. It had bakeries and kitchens, pantries, butteries and wine cellars, and even its own brewery. Standing proudly amid all this was the priory church, and you can see how grand it must once have been by looking at its magnificent west front today. Its dimensions are cathedral-like, with some of the most ornate carving anywhere in the county. There were also dormitories and refectories, and – something children seem to find fascinating – a long, multi-seated latrine set over a small stream.

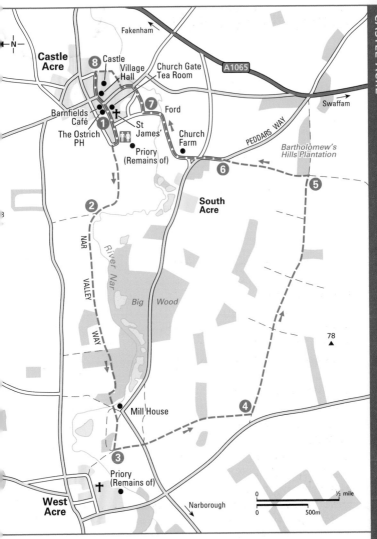

1 From the green, walk along the lane past St James' Church until you reach the entrance to the priory. Bear right around the corner and then left, after a few paces, down the wide track signed 'Nar Valley Way'. Continue until you reach a bend of the River Nar.

2 At the river, turn left and go through the kissing gate along the trail waymarked with a Nar Valley Way disk. Walk alongside a hedge past a wet meadow, with the River Nar to your left, and enter a wood. Keep to this grassy track, continuing through the wood until you reach a gate. Cross the footbridge and keep straight ahead along a boardwalk to another footbridge over the River Nar, with the old Mill House on your left. When you reach a lane with a ford on your right, go straight across to the signed path opposite and walk along a woodland track, looking for glimpses of West Acre priory ruins ahead to the left across fields.

3 Just before reaching a large gate, turn sharp left along a footpath that leads across fields alongside a fence and a hedge. The ruins of West Acre priory are clearly visible to the right. Follow this footpath for 0.25 miles (400m) until you reach a lane. Cross the lane and take the footpath opposite (not the bridleway on your left). Go up a hill, under power lines and past a wood. At the crest of the hill you reach a junction.

4 Turn left onto the bridleway and continue straight ahead at two crossroads. Look for deer and shy game birds, and note the prairie-style fields to the left and right.

5 Turn left at the third crossroads, onto an ancient drove road used in Roman times, passing Bartholomew's Hills Plantation on your right. Keep walking uphill along this sandy track until you see Castle Acre Priory and St James' Church through the trees ahead. As you descend, go under the power lines again, and meet a lane at the foot of the hill.

6 Go straight ahead on the lane, which is part of the Peddars Way. At the next junction go straight on again, down the lane marked 'Ford – Deep Water'. Walk past Church Farm on your right to reach a pebble-bottomed river and a ford. Through the trees you will glimpse splendid views of the priory to your left. Cross the river and continue walking along this tiny lane until you see an acorn sign marking the Peddars Way.

7 Turn right along the Peddars Way and keep walking straight ahead until you see a sign for Blind Lane, just after another road joins from the left. Turn left at the junction, then right into Cuckstool Lane, with the castle to your left. Follow the grassy path, which skirts around the castle bailey, climbing steeply to arrive at a lane.

8 Turn left and walk along the lane, past the village hall and old Bailey gate, to the village green.

WHERE TO EAT AND DRINK There are several good lunch options on the village green at Castle Acre. The Ostrich has a beer garden and offers a range of good food and ales. Barnfields Café serves home-made soup, sandwiches, pies and cakes in a beautiful walled garden in summer. Further along the green is the Church Gate Tea Room.

WHAT TO SEE The Prior's Lodging is the best of the buildings in the Castle Acre Priory complex. It was built in the 12th century, but was added to during the next 800 years and is in a remarkable state of preservation. After the monastery was destroyed, it was used as a house for the bailiff of the Coke Estate.

WHILE YOU'RE THERE Visit All Saints' Church, Narborough, 5 miles (8km) northwest of Swaffham. Here you will see the monument to Clement Spelman (d.1679), who was so proud that he insisted on being buried upright so no one would walk over him. The Victorians opened the tomb and found the coffin was indeed on its end.

Brancaster Staithe and Branodunum

DISTANCE 4.5 miles (7.2km)   MINIMUM TIME 2hrs 15min

ASCENT/GRADIENT 148ft (45m) ▲▲▲   LEVEL OF DIFFICULTY +++

PATHS Winding paths and tracks, with some paved lanes

LANDSCAPE Salt marshes, mudflats, farmland and common

SUGGESTED MAP AA Walker's Map 21 North Norfolk Coast

START/FINISH Grid reference: TF793443

DOG FRIENDLINESS On lead in nature reserves and farmland; note dog-free areas on beaches

PARKING Near National Trust's Dial House or in lay-by on A149 on edge of Brancaster Staithe

PUBLIC TOILETS None on route

Some time around AD 240–250 the Romans came to Brancaster and built a fort. It was square with a tower at each corner. Between the towers was a curtain wall about 10ft (3m) thick, and there was a gate halfway along each of the four walls. In addition to this, they added a wide ditch, so that any attackers would have to climb down it and up the other side – all the while bombarded with arrows and stones from the defenders above. They reinforced the walls by adding a rampart inside.

THE ROMAN FORT OF BRANODUNUM

The fort of Branodunum was quite large – about 6.5 acres (2.6ha), and was probably built over a site that had been levelled by previous occupants. Although it lies in a field that is about a mile (1.6km) from the sea today, when the Romans built their fort it was right on the estuary. It was a fabulous location, providing good access to the sea, and close to the Peddars Way, an important line of communication.

By the 4th century, the civilian population that relied on the fort's protection had moved away from Branodunum. The military settlement survived for a while as the most northerly of the Saxon Shore fort systems designed to protect the Dalmatian cavalry against Anglo-Saxon raids, but eventually it was abandoned. Little remains except for some earthworks covered in vegetation, but walking around the field will give you an idea of its size.

RESERVED FOR WILDFOWL

The site is now in the care of the National Trust, which owns around 2,000 acres (810ha) of the coast, including 4 miles (6.4km) of tidal foreshore. The entire region, with its salt marshes, mudflats and sand dunes, is a haven for birds, including common and Sandwich terns.

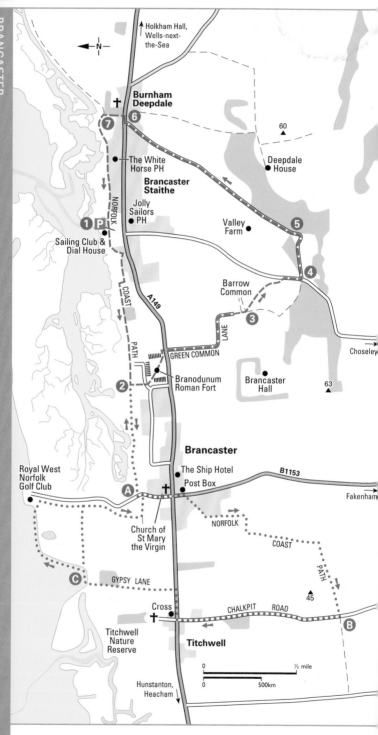

↑ Holkham Hall,
Wells-next-
the-Sea

← N →

✝ **Burnham
Deepdale**

⑦

⑥

● The White
Horse PH

**Brancaster
Staithe**

Jolly
Sailors
● PH

60
▲

Deepdale
● House

① P

Sailing Club &
Dial House

NORFOLK

Valley
Farm ●

⑤

COAST

A149

Barrow
Common

④

③

LANE

GREEN COMMON

PATH

② ▥

▥ Branodunum
Roman Fort

Brancaster
Hall ●

63
▲

Choseley →

Brancaster

● The Ship Hotel

● Post Box

B1153

Royal West
Norfolk
Golf Club

●

Ⓐ

✝

Fakenham →

Church of
St Mary
the Virgin

NORFOLK

COAST

Ⓒ

GYPSY LANE

PATH

Cross
✝

CHALKPIT ROAD

45
▲

Ⓑ

Titchwell
Nature
Reserve

Titchwell

0   ½ mile

0   500km

Hunstanton,
Heacham
↓

1 Walk into the area owned by the Sailing Club and, just before the slipway, you will see the National Trail marker on your left. Go through the kissing gate and stroll along the boardwalk edging the marshes. Continue ahead and pass a brick and flint house.

2 Turn left and leave the coastal path, going through a kissing gate to enter a large field with an interpretive sign about Branodunum. This is Rack Hill, the area that houses the Roman fort. Follow the right-hand side of the field until you reach another kissing gate. Cross the lane through another kissing gate. Head for the opposite left corner of the field. You can follow the path to either left or right around the field edge, or cut straight across the middle. Go through the kissing gate and cross the A149 onto Green Common Lane. The track bends twice, but follow it until it comes to a gate and footpath junction to your left. Continue straight along the grassy track between the hedges.

3 Here you enter Barrow Common nature reserve. At the seat you have the choice of three paths. Take the middle one, and keep straight on as you pass other junctions. You will eventually exit onto a peaceful paved lane. Turn right and follow the lane down a fairly steep hill.

4 Turn left at the junction. Across from here, during the early summer, are fields of poppies. Continue until you reach a wood, where you may hear the lilting song of nightingales.

5 The road bends sharply left, and a short section of footpath allows you to cut the corner. The road has a broad, grassy verge you can walk on for most of the way.

6 Cross the A149 with care and turn right. After a few paces take the first left down The Drove, opposite the garage and post office. At the end of the lane is a sign for the coast path. Follow it down a narrow, tree-lined track until it emerges onto marshes and the main Norfolk Coast Path.

7 Turn left and walk along the path until you see the yacht masts of the Sailing Club. Reach a small boatyard, then follow the trail through wooden huts. The next buildings are home to the Sailing Club itself, before you reach the car park.

WHERE TO EAT AND DRINK The Jolly Sailors in Brancaster Staithe serves bar meals and has a restaurant, a sea view, and is open daily. Further along the road towards Burnham Deepdale is The White Horse, with its bar and conservatory restaurant with deck terrace. At Brancaster, The Ship opposite the church has a pleasant garden. Families are welcome, and there are bar meals and a restaurant.

WHAT TO SEE Scolt Head Island nature reserve and bird sanctuary lies about 1 mile (1.6km) to the north.

WHILE YOU'RE THERE Norfolk Lavender in nearby Heacham is one of England's finest lavender farms. It is open all year, and there is a shop and a tea room. In the opposite direction is Holkham Hall and its Bygones Museum.

From Brancaster to Titchwell

DISTANCE 7.25 miles (11.7km)   MINIMUM TIME 3hrs

ASCENT/GRADIENT 174ft (53m) ▲▲▲   LEVEL OF DIFFICULTY ✚✚✚

SEE MAP AND INFORMATION PANEL FOR WALK 38

From outside Brancaster Staithe Sailing Club, take the Norfolk Coast Path west, as with Walk 38. Continue on the boadwalk past Point **②**, to reach an information sign about the Branodunum Roman fort on your left. The salt marshes stretch out to your right, and in the distance, the clubhouse of the Royal West Norfolk Golf Club, which you'll pass later on.

Cross a stile with steel railing and a concrete step. The path broadens out into a track – at the junction (Point **Ⓐ**) follow the signpost left for the Norfolk Coast Path. Pass the Church of St Mary the Virgin, and immediately after cross the A149 coast road. After a few steps, take Choseley Road, which forks to the right opposite the post box. It starts out as a narrow lane flanked by flint cottages and then by tall hedges. It bends at right angles, to the right, then left, to gain some height and enjoy panoramic views of the coast.

Where the climb levels off, the track turns 90-degrees right, with a Norfolk Coast Path waymarker to keep you on track. Ahead you can see some farm buildings and a mobile phone mast, but before you reach them, turn right, Point **Ⓑ**, leaving the Norfolk Coast Path. You are now on a small, paved lane, Chalkpit Road.

At the crossroads with the A149, turn right. Walk along the left-hand pavement, and just after a speed de-restriction sign, turn left onto Gypsy Lane, a small well-defined footpath through woods.

Walk through this tunnel of foliage, until it opens out to a coastal embankment, with Titchwell Nature Reserve (RSPB) to your left. Follow the embankment round to Brancaster Ford, Point **Ⓒ**. Where you go from here depends on the tide. The main route goes ahead, off the embankment and following the path to the dunes and the golf clubhouse beyond. If there is water running over the ford, turn right and stay on the embankment.

The main route skirts along the beach to reach a sandy track to the right of the golf club. Now follow the path south along the top of the embankment. At the end of the path, drop down to bushes and scrub before turning left onto a track. At the junction with a road which comes from the golf club, jink left and immediately right, Point **Ⓐ**. From here follow the Norfolk Coast Path back to Brancaster Staithe.

Exploring the Massinghams

DISTANCE 4.75 miles (7.7km)	MINIMUM TIME 2hrs

ASCENT/GRADIENT 115ft (35m) ▲▲▲   LEVEL OF DIFFICULTY ✚✚✚

PATHS Country lanes, tracks and footpaths

LANDSCAPE Gently rolling farmland and common

SUGGESTED MAP OS Explorer 250 Norfolk Coast West

START/FINISH Grid reference: TF972241

DOG FRIENDLINESS Lead required along roads and in village centre

PARKING On road outside church in Little Massingham

PUBLIC TOILETS None on route

In medieval times Norfolk and Suffolk were among the most densely populated and important regions in England. Today, Norfolk is one of the least populated counties and rural depopulation in particular has been a problem, with people moving out of the villages to work elsewhere.

Evidence of a more prosperous era in Norfolk's history can be seen in the huge number of ruined priories and abbeys that are scattered across it. One of these was the Augustinian priory that was founded at Great Massingham in the early 1200s. The canons evidently saw the fertile land, conveniently located on an ancient line of communication, the Peddars Way, and decided it was a good place for a small community to live. Today very little survives of what was probably a set of handsome buildings and a small forest called Hartswood. There are some fragments of masonry in and around Abbey Farm and a few woodland plants have survived the clearing of the forest.

ST MARY'S CHURCH

St Mary's Church, which stands on the green at Great Massingham, has a splendid 15th-century tower and a 13th-century porch, and its interior depicts a menagerie of carved animals standing guard over the south aisle. The great stone tower of this church, which is visible for many miles across the local countryside, was once an important landmark for pilgrims navigating their way on foot or horseback to the shrine at nearby Walsingham. In medieval times, when the shrine was at the height of its popularity, Great Massingham did rather well out of weary travellers who wanted a bed for the night and a hot meal. Sir Robert Walpole, who went on to become Britain's first Prime Minister, received part of his early education in St Mary's Church – its porch was once used as the village school room.

PONDS AND PUBS

The large village ponds that make Great Massingham so distinctive probably have their origins as the fish ponds for the former Augustinian abbey that stood nearby. The ponds serve a less practical purpose these days, but continue to provide a haven for a variety of waterfowl. The Dabbling Duck on the green celebrates this with its name, but this pub, formerly the Rose and Crown, is the sole survivor of as many as five that use to serve the village.

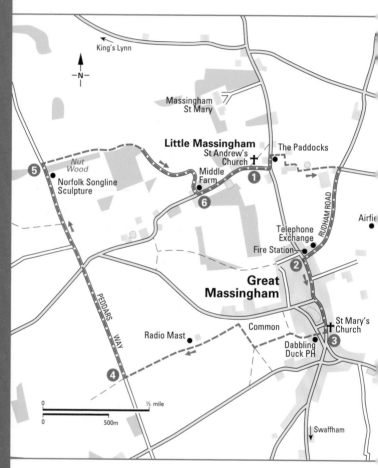

① From St Andrew's Church in Little Massingham walk towards the post box. Go to the end of the lane and turn left at the T-junction. After a few steps you reach a farm, The Paddocks, on your right. Turn right along the driveway and follow the track that winds round farm buildings. You will know you are on the public footpath when you pass the pond on your left. The track soon reaches a junction at Rudham Road, where you turn right towards Great Massingham. Go up a small hill between hedgerows, and stay on this road as it bends right, passing a telephone exchange and allotments to arrive at a fire station and junction.

2 Cross over and turn left to walk on the footpath. This is Great Massingham. One of its inhabitants in the 16th century was Stephen Perse, who later studied medicine at Gonville and Caius College in Cambridge. He founded a school there, called The Perse, which still thrives. The road eventually reaches a charming village green complete with duck pond. St Mary's Church stands on the green nearby.

3 Walk across the green towards the sign for Abbey Road. Next to this is a signposted track leading up the side of the quaintly named Hoss-Chestnut House. This will bring you out on to the rather wild common, where the foundations of the priory (it was never an abbey, despite its name) are supposed to be, although they are almost impossible to find. Follow the path alongside the common, aiming for the tall radio mast ahead of you. The path turns right alongside a field to arrive at a paved track. Turn left here, passing the radio mast and water tower. Once you have reached the mast the track becomes pleasantly rural and the verges are full of red campion and delicate violets in early spring.

4 This track meets the Peddars Way, which is well signposted. Turn right, and continue walking along this straight track for about a mile (1.6km). This bisects a huge field landscape and climbs to reach about 300ft (91m) above sea level, while mature oak trees rustle their leaves in the breeze. Cross a road and keep straight ahead on the Peddars Way. Ignore a private track and the public bridleway to your left and continue until you reach a bridleway on the right, just after a Norfolk Songlines sculpture evoking images of an ancient land and the walkers who have used this path before.

5 Turn right with the trees of Nut Wood to your right and rolling fields to your left. Keep right when you reach another track and follow it between tall hedgerows and through Middle Farm to reach a quiet lane.

6 Turn left here. A lake, perhaps with squabbling moorhens, lies to your right. The lane ascends a hill and you will find yourself back at St Andrew's Church in Little Massingham again.

WHERE TO EAT AND DRINK The Dabbling Duck in Great Massingham is the last of the village's six pubs. Formerly the Rose and Crown, it closed in 2001 and was bought by the local council. It reopened in 2006 and is now a thriving pub serving seasonal produce and real ales, with a beer garden, children's play area and a terrace overlooking the green.

WHILE YOU'RE THERE Sandringham House and gardens (see Walk 41) and the Norman keep at Castle Rising (see Walk 43) are within easy reach of the Massinghams. Castle Acre castle and priory (see Walk 37) are also a short drive away. Since the Peddars Way passes just to the west of the village, this is also a good place to start the long distance Peddars Way and Norfolk Coast Path National Trail.

Sandringham and Wolferton

DISTANCE 6.5 miles (10.4km)	MINIMUM TIME 3hrs

ASCENT/GRADIENT 213ft (65m) ▲▲▲   LEVEL OF DIFFICULTY ✦✦✦

PATHS Marked forest trails and country lanes, some steps

LANDSCAPE Country park and woodland nature reserve

SUGGESTED MAP AA Walker's Map 21 North Norfolk Coast

START/FINISH Grid reference: TF668280

DOG FRIENDLINESS Dogs should be kept on lead in nature reserves

PARKING Scissors Cross car park on road to Wolferton

PUBLIC TOILETS At Sandringham visitor centre

In 1862 revenues from the Duchy of Cornwall had raised such a large sum of money for its owner, the Prince of Wales – the future King Edward VII – that he was able to buy himself a fine house. He chose Sandringham, set in some 7,000 acres (2,835ha) of beautiful rolling countryside. The house, however, was not at all to his liking, so he set about rebuilding it in a style he felt reflected his status. The result was the rambling Jacobean-style palace in red brick and stone that you can visit today – providing that no member of the royal family is in residence, of course.

Today it is the private property of the Queen, along with much of the surrounding countryside. In 1968 she expressed the wish that the general public should also enjoy the estate and some 600 acres (243ha) of woodland and open heath were set aside as the Sandringham Country Park. Access to the park is free (there is a charge to enter Sandringham Gardens) and visitors can enjoy the peaceful waymarked nature trails, as well as the observation hide to watch the wildlife around Jocelyn's Wood nature reserve. Visitors to the house and its gardens can also see some of the most spectacular parkland in the country, with an intriguing mixture of formal arrangements and ancient rambling woodland.

When Sandringham was owned by the fun-loving Prince of Wales, the unassuming little railway station at nearby Wolferton saw some of the world's most powerful monarchs and statesmen pass through the station. In 1898 the track from King's Lynn was upgraded and two staterooms were added to the station, so that visiting dignitaries could arrive in style. When the railways came under the axe in the 1960s, Wolferton looked set to follow the fate of many other small stations, but one British Rail inspector was so impressed by what he saw that he decided to buy it. Painstaking restoration took place and the waiting rooms were converted into a museum. Unfortunately, the Sandringham Estate refused permission for the museum to put up new advertising signs, so in 2001 the owner decided to sell up. It's now a private house, but the fabric remains and the pretty rust-red ironstone station, easily seen from the road, is close to how it might have looked in the 19th century. There are no rail tracks, and flowers enjoy the place where grunting, hissing steam engines would once have stood.

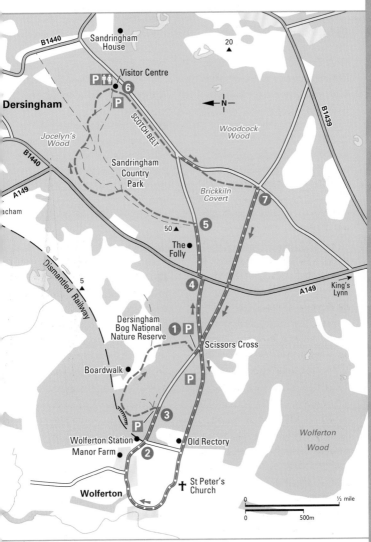

● Cross the road from the car park and bear right on the lane towards Wolferton. The walled gardens of the Old Rectory mark the end of the mixed woodland. Continue

straight ahead at the junction, past St Peter's Church. The road bends to the right, passing the old railway gatehouse and cottages (1881) bearing the fleur-de-lis emblem.

Stay on this road to make a complete circuit of the village, eventually arriving at Wolferton Station.

2 After the station, follow the road to the left and go up a hill until you reach the car park for the Dersingham nature reserve and a gate beyond it.

3 Go through the gate and take the track to your left, signed 'Clifftop Stroll'. The path climbs to a cliff top looking out over a forest, which 6,000 years ago was the seabed (now 1.5miles/2.4km distant). Follow the track until you see the 330yd (302m) circular boardwalk around the bog below you. Walk down the steps to explore the bog walk. Emerging from the boardwalk, take the sandy track to your left until you can bear right onto a path signposted back to Scissors Cross car park. Take the left fork out of the car park and walk along this road to the A149.

4 Cross the A149 and take the lane opposite, passing a house named The Folly. After a few paces you will see a lane to your left which is marked 'scenic drive'. Turn left to walk through the gates.

5 Walk along the drive or take the footpath on the right through Sandringham Country Park. When you see a processional avenue leading to Sandringham House on your right, leave the drive and look for a gap in the trees to your left. Follow the trail past a bench and down some steps, then stay on the yellow trail (waymarked in the opposite direction) as it winds through Jocelyn's Wood before returning to the main drive. Turn left and walk along the drive to the car park and visitor centre.

6 From the visitor centre, head for the lower car park and pick up the yellow trail again, which follows the main road, but is tucked away behind the trees of Scotch Belt. Cross a lane, then take the road ahead to your left for 200yds (183m) before picking up the path on your right as it passes through Brickkiln Covert.

7 At the crossroads, where the footpath comes to an end, turn right down a quiet lane with wide verges. You are still in woodland, although the trees here tend to be silver birch rather than the oaks and pines seen earlier. Cross the A149 to reach Scissors Cross.

WHERE TO EAT AND DRINK The Sandringham Visitor Centre is open every day except Good Friday and Christmas Day, though the house and gardens are closed in winter. There is a self-service restaurant, a tea room and kiosks selling sandwiches, snacks and ice cream.

WHAT TO SEE It is well worth taking the time to follow the boardwalk into Dersingham Bog. This is circular, and in the summer you can expect to see seven or eight species of sphagnum moss, black sedge, cottongrass, sundew and bog asphodel.

WHILE YOU'RE THERE This walk will take you through the country park, but not into the Sandringham Estate, where you must pay an entrance fee. The fee includes access to the gardens with their own woodland walks, the house and the museum. The museum has vintage royal coaches and cars, a large collection of historic photographs and a sad tribute to the Sandringham Company, who died in the Gallipoli campaign in 1915.

Right: Sandringham House, surrounded by attractive gardens and a lake (Walk 41)

Old Hunstanton's Dunes

DISTANCE 8 miles (12.9km)   MINIMUM TIME 3hrs 30min

ASCENT/GRADIENT 164ft (50m) ▲▲▲   LEVEL OF DIFFICULTY +++

PATHS Country tracks, lanes, muddy paths and sand dunes

LANDSCAPE Sandy beaches, rolling chalk valleys and farmland

SUGGESTED MAP AA Walker's Map 21 North Norfolk Coast

START/FINISH Grid reference: TF697438

DOG FRIENDLINESS On lead in nature reserves and on farmland

PARKING Beach car park at Holme next the Sea (pay at kiosk)

PUBLIC TOILETS By beach car park

Old Hunstanton is steeped in history and legend. It is said that St Edmund was shipwrecked here in AD 855, and was so grateful for being spared a watery death in the Wash that he built a chapel as an act of thanksgiving. The 13th-century ruins still stand today, looking out across grey stormy seas from near the old lighthouse. Edmund left Hunstanton soon after and went on to become King of the East Angles. Between AD 869 and 870 Vikings invaded his kingdom and fought battles until he was captured. He refused to renounce his faith and died a particularly unpleasant death.

Some years later, Edmund's grave was dug up and his body was found to be uncorrupted. It was declared a miracle, and his remains were moved around the country for many years in an attempt to keep them safe from Vikings. They were eventually kept in Bury St Edmunds, although records are vague about what happened to them later. Some say they were taken to France, while others claim he was reinterred at Bury after the Reformation. Regardless of the fate of the relics, Hunstanton is proud of its claim to a small piece of the saint's history.

Edmund is not the only remarkable historical figure to be associated with the village. Members of the Le Strange family have been squires and landlords here for more than 800 years. They laid claim to the beach and, according to one charter, all that is in the sea for as far as a horseman can hurl a spear at low tide. The family still hold the title of Lord High Admiral of the Wash. There is a popular local story that tells of a famous German lady swimmer called Mercedes Gleitze performing the impressive feat of swimming the Wash from Lincolnshire to Norfolk in the 1930s and the admiral promptly stepping forward to claim her as his rightful property!

The lighthouse that has become a symbol of this attractive town dates from 1840. When World War I broke out in 1914, the light was extinguished and was never lit again. The lighthouse is now in private

Left: Erosion on the cliffs at Hunstanton (Walk 42)

hands. Because of its strategic position on the coast, Hunstanton was the site of some very clandestine happenings in that war. Hippisley Hut, a bungalow, was used to house a secret listening post to monitor the activities of German Zeppelins, and some of its secrets remain hidden even today.

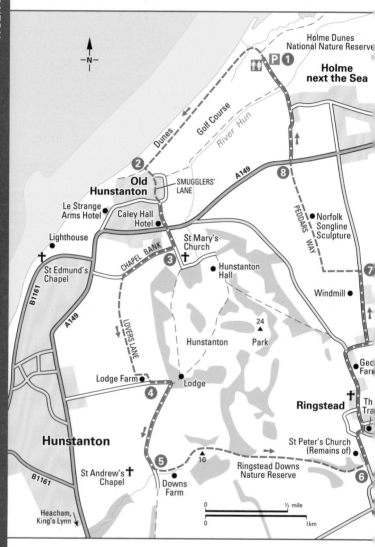

❶ Walk towards the sea and turn left to head across the dunes. This is Norfolk at its best, with miles of sandy beaches and dunes, and the lighthouse at Old Hunstanton visible on a cliff. Keep close to the golf course and after about a mile (1.6km) you will arrive at a colourful row of beach huts.

❷ When you see a gap in the fence to your left, take the path across the golf course and continue straight ahead into Smugglers' Lane. Emerging at a junction, take the lane opposite, past the post box to reach Caley Hall Hotel. Cross the A149 and aim for the road signed 'To St Mary's Church', where you can see the grave of William Green, shot by smugglers.

3 Turn right up Chapel Bank, through a tunnel of shade, before reaching open farmland. After 700yds (640m), turn left on a grassy track, Lovers Lane, a permissive path. When you reach Lodge Farm, follow the track around farm buildings to a lane.

4 Turn left along the lane. When you see the fairy-tale lodge of Hunstanton Park ahead, follow the lane round to the right along an avenue of mature trees. In the field to your right you will see the ruins of 13th-century St Andrew's Chapel.

5 Bear left at Downs Farm and head for the gate to enter Ringstead Downs Nature Reserve, one of just a few

areas in Norfolk that is chalk rather than sand. It belongs to the Norfolk Wildlife Trust and the area is grazed by traditional hill sheep. This is one of the most beautiful parts of the walk. Follow the path right through the reserve until you reach a lane.

6 Turn left into Ringstead, where the tower of St Peter's Church still stands. Stay on this road as it bends right and left through the village, passing The Gin Trap Inn. The road climbs gently out of the village, forking right then left along the Peddars Way towards a sail-less windmill.

7 At the last house, look for the waymarked path to the left. This follows a field boundary, then turns right into a lovely tunnel of hedges. Note the Norfolk Songline sculpture halfway along the path.

8 Cross the A149 and walk through Holme village, with its long green, to reach the car park.

WHERE TO EAT AND DRINK The Caley Hall Hotel (1648) has a good restaurant. In summer, you can take afternoon tea on the patio. Bar meals are also available at the Ancient Mariner Inn, attached to the Le Strange Arms Hotel in Old Hunstanton. The kiosk at the car park is open all summer and on winter weekends, selling bacon and sausage rolls, ice cream and snacks. If you want to break your walk halfway, The Gin Trap Inn at Ringstead makes a good lunch stop.

WHAT TO SEE The Ringstead Downs Nature Reserve is home to rock roses, meadow grasshoppers and gorse. While walking along the dunes stop to look at the marram grass. This durable plant is used to stabilise the sand, and to prevent it from being scoured away by the fierce winds that roar in from the North Sea.

WHILE YOU'RE THERE Holmes Dunes National Nature Reserve is 474 acres (192ha) of sand dunes, foreshore and salt marsh, particularly favoured by winter migrants. Although these birds can start to arrive as early as July, the peak time is October and November. It is a spectacular sight to see thousands of birds arriving from the North Sea on a clear autumn morning. They rest and feed, then move on to milder climes and make their return journeys around March.

A Circuit from Castle Rising

DISTANCE 7 miles (11.3km)   MINIMUM TIME 3hrs

ASCENT/GRADIENT 131ft (40m) ▲▲▲   LEVEL OF DIFFICULTY ✚✚✚

PATHS Some country lanes, but mostly footpaths

LANDSCAPE Woodland, farmland, heath and meadow

SUGGESTED MAP AA Leisure Map 6 North West Norfolk

START/FINISH Grid reference: TF666244

DOG FRIENDLINESS Dogs are restricted in nature reserves

PARKING English Heritage Castle Rising car park (check opening times at www.english-heritage.org.uk) or on lane outside church

PUBLIC TOILETS At car park

Castle Rising has a magnificent Norman castle, complete with narrow corridors, unexpected little chambers and a small chapel embedded in its ramparts. There is also a sturdy 12th-century village church with a peaceful graveyard and a picturesque former post office (now a tea room). And there is a pleasant pub, pretty traditional carrstone (red sandstone) cottages, delightful almshouses and a fascinating history. Who could want more?

The castle has a great deal to offer, starting with its awesome banks and ditches, its half-buried Norman chapel and its two wells. But the most impressive feature is undoubtedly the keep, a squat, rectangular tower that stands some 50ft (15m) high. The blind arcading (a series of arches on a wall) that decorates its front would not be out of place on a grand cathedral.

QUEEN ISABELLA

Castle Rising's best known incumbent was Isabella, wife of Edward II. Not for nothing was she known as the 'She-Wolf of France'. She was intelligent and power-hungry and soon tired of her ineffectual (and probably homosexual) husband. She joined forces with her lover, Roger Mortimer, to depose and murder Edward, and enjoyed several years effectively ruling the country while her son, Edward III, was in his minority. However, no man wants his mother looking over his shoulder while he tries to rule a kingdom, and Isabella was gently prised from the court and sent to live in her various castles once Edward came of age. One of these was Rising.

The real story about Isabella and Castle Rising has been distorted and many tales have Isabella banished from Edward III's court to languish as a prisoner here for 27 years, before her death in 1358. The truth is rather different. The monarchy could not afford to acknowledge that the King's mother was instrumental in murdering his father and so the incident was covered up. After 1331, Isabella did spend more time in her role as Dowager Queen and less time trying to influence affairs of state, but she was never a prisoner. She lived in great luxury, moving with her vast army of servants from one place to another, like any wealthy lady of her age.

Isabella seems to have enjoyed life at Castle Rising. Archaeological evidence shows that new buildings were raised during her time, including a residential suite with its own chapel.

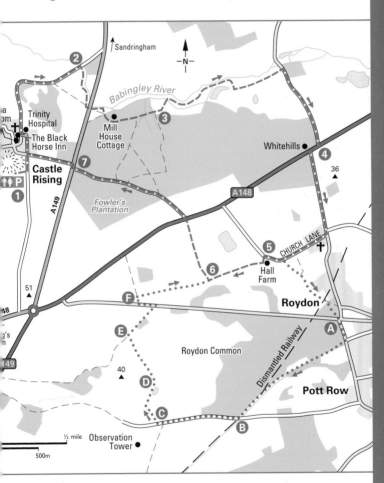

❶ Leave the car park, turn left to walk downhill and go straight ahead at the crossroads, passing cottages built of carrstone. After the road bends left, take the lane to your right between Trinity Hospital and the church. Continue through a set of gates and follow the road around a bend, Onion Corner, named after the aroma of wild garlic in spring. Continue to a bridge with white railings.

② Take the path to the right through a grassy meadow, with Babingley River to your left. Cross the A149 to the stile opposite. Climb a second stile and follow the path across a meadow. Cross another stile, then turn right to emerge on a gravel lane near the entrance to Mill House. Keep straight ahead and stay on this lane, ignoring footpath signs to the right, as it bends left to Mill House Cottage. Take the wide grassy track signposted to the right opposite the cottage, passing a ruined barn. The track passes through the woods, then crosses a bright orange stream, stained by dissolved iron-rich rocks.

③ Bear left across the open meadow in front of you, heading for the opposite corner. Turn right here and follow the footpath signs along the banks of the Babingley River. Nettles can be a problem, as can boggy ground underfoot. Cross one stile and then a second by a wooden footbridge and continue along the river bank, then follow the path round to the right and cross another stile before turning left along a wide field-edge track with a stream on the left. Turn right when you reach a paved lane and follow this to the A148.

④ Turn right at the A148, then walk along the verge on the opposite side until you reach the first lane on your left. Turn left and follow the road uphill to enter Roydon. Turn right at the village sign into Church Lane. The church has a marvellous Romanesque south door. Continue out of the village until Church Lane bends to the right, to a green-gated lane.

⑤ Turn left onto the green-gated lane, following signs for Sunnyside Veterinary Clinic. After a few yards turn right onto a track signposted as a public footpath. Follow this for about 700yds (640m) until you meet another public footpath found on the right.

⑥ Turn right and follow this sandy track until you reach the A148. Take the minor road opposite, which has oak trees that grow progressively larger as you walk further from the main road. By the time you reach Fowler's Plantation, they tower above you.

⑦ Cross the A149 and walk down the lane opposite to return to Castle Rising. Turn left up the lane marked towards the castle, then right, to the car park.

WHERE TO EAT AND DRINK The Black Horse Inn, Castle Rising, is pleasantly situated near the church and serves good food seven days a week. The Castle Rising Tea Room in the former post office is a lovely place for cake and tea and has a pretty garden.

WHAT TO SEE You walk past the Hospital of the Holy and Undivided Trinity as you leave Castle Rising. This is open to visitors at certain times and is well worth a look. The building dates from the 17th century, and was originally intended as almshouses for 'needy women of good character'. Fallow and roe deer are common in the woods around the walk, and you may glimpse red squirrels.

WHILE YOU'RE THERE Just 5 miles (8km) away is King's Lynn (see Walk 46) with its fascinating architecture, Lynn Museum and Old Gaol House Museum. Sandringham House and country park are located to the north (see Walk 41).

Roydon Common Reserve

DISTANCE 10.5 miles (16.9km)   MINIMUM TIME 4hrs 15min

ASCENT/GRADIENT 197ft (60m) ▲▲▲   LEVEL OF DIFFICULTY +++

SEE MAP AND INFORMATION PANEL FOR WALK 43

Roydon Common is a relic of the ancient grazing areas that once covered much of the county, and it offers a variety of habitats for plants and animals. Most of it is dry heath, where species like heathers thrive on sandy soil. Carr is the wettest habitat, and plants such as willow and birch offer shade to mosses and ferns below. Mire is peaty soil that gathers in the valley bottom and is a good place to spot bog asphodel.

When Church Lane bends to the right just before Point ❺, take the signposted restricted byway to your left, along a grassy track between two hedges with a sunken feel to it. When you reach the modern bungalow, cross the track and go through the metal gate in front of you. Cross the meadow full of bog-loving plants, go through a second gate and walk beside a factory to enter a rough common of gorse and hawthorn. Approximately 30yds (27m) after entering the trees, branch right onto a path that becomes progressively better defined until it emerges at a crossroads, Point ❹.

Cross the road, go down Chapel Road and take the footpath to your right, opposite Chequers Road. The path threads for a little less than a mile (1.6km) beside a stream, with Roydon Common off to your right.

The woodland is mixed, with mature beech, silver birch, oak and alder.

Go through a gate at Point ❸, and turn right past the white timber-clad Railway Gatehouse. The light sandy soil of Grimston Warren to your left was a tempting area for growing conifers, but these were removed in 2000 and the area has been restored to heathland.

Ahead, the stark remains of a World War II observation tower dominate the latest area of heathland restoration. Soon after passing a track leading off to the left, turn right on a footpath into Roydon Common National Nature Reserve, Point ❸. As you climb to reach Point ❹ there are lovely views to your right across a field of heather marked by scrubby trees. When you reach an orange-brown mud road, turn right, Point ❸, leaving the nature reserve and continuing to the main road.

Turn left and walk 150yds (137m) along the verge until you reach a line of Scots pines. Go past these, then take the track immediately to your right, Point ❺. Go through the first gap on your right and you will see a 'Norfolk Walks' waymark sign. Walk along this path until you reach Point ❻, where you turn left to rejoin the main route.

Around Oxburgh Hall

DISTANCE 3.25 miles (5.3km)	MINIMUM TIME 1hr 30min

ASCENT/GRADIENT Negligible ▲▲▲   LEVEL OF DIFFICULTY ✚✚✚

PATHS Footpaths and country lanes

LANDSCAPE National Trust house and arable farmland

SUGGESTED MAP OS Explorer 236 King's Lynn, Downham Market & Swaffham

START/FINISH Grid reference: TF743015

DOG FRIENDLINESS Can run free, but must be under control on farmland

PARKING On-street parking around village green and car park at Bedingfeld Arms

PUBLIC TOILETS None on route

Oxburgh Hall is one of Norfolk's greatest treasures. It is a gorgeous cluster of red-brick buildings standing defiantly inside a wide moat. These days the moat contains nothing more threatening than carp and water lilies, but the Bedingfeld family, who have owned the house since the 15th century, had good cause to protect themselves in the past. They have demonstrated loyalty to two causes – the Catholic Church and the English Crown – both of which have led them into considerable danger. The pub in Oxborough village is named after the family.

A PRIEST'S HIDING PLACE

The Bedingfelds' loyalty to their religion stood them in good stead until Tudor times, but was a dangerous position to hold during the Reformation – as the 16th-century Priest Hole attests. When it became illegal to hold Catholic Masses, some wealthy families were reduced to building secret places in their homes, so that their household priest could hide there, occasionally for some considerable time, without being detected. Oxburgh Hall was one such house.

RISE AND FALL

Before the Dissolution of the Monasteries, the Bedingfelds were a respected and influential family. One member was so trusted by Henry VIII that he was given the divorced Catherine of Aragon to watch over and his son was entrusted with the care of the future Elizabeth I. However, as Protestantism became more firmly rooted, the Bedingfelds fell from favour.

They fell even further during the Civil War when they remained firmly Royalist. Their allegiance to Charles I saw Oxburgh Hall occupied and damaged by Roundheads. They survived until the Restoration, when their fortunes turned again and they began to claw back some of their power and riches.

Among the Hall's finest treasures are its Marian wall hangings. These tapestries were sewn sometime around 1570 by Mary, Queen of Scots, and the Countess of Shrewsbury, Bess of Hardwick.

Oxburgh Hall has seen many changes since Sir Edmund Bedingfeld applied for a licence to crenellate – to upgrade his manor defensively – in 1482, but, conversely, many things have remained unaltered. Edmund's great gatehouse still dominates the house, and Pugin's restoration in the 1830s was sympathetic to the original style. Between 1835 and 1839 a chapel was built in the grounds of the hall, near the gatehouse. In 1845 the French gardens were laid out. In 1952 it was acquired by the National Trust. Visitors today can enjoy strolls around the kitchen garden and orchard, and explore the woodland.

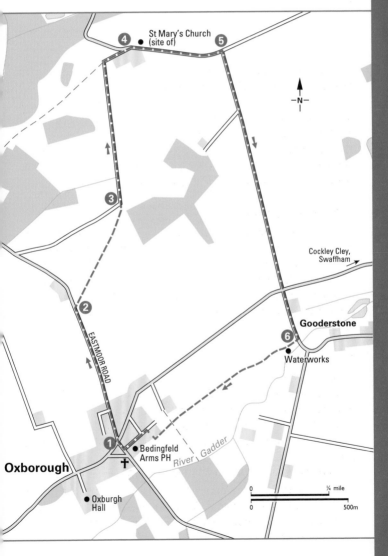

1 Begin by walking up Eastmoor Road, opposite the church. Then, after about 700yds (640m), take the footpath to your right.

2 The signed path may be partially obscured by crops, but take a diagonal direction north until you reach the end of the second field.

3 Turn left along a sandy farm track with a line of trees to your right. After about 800yds (732m), the track bends right to meet a road beside a barn.

4 Turn right, with the earthworks of old St Mary's Church in the field to your left.

5 After about 600yds (549m), the lane bends sharp right towards Gooderstone and Oxborough. Follow this road to a crossroads. Go straight across, down the road marked 'Weak bridge'.

6 Look for the footpath marked on your right, which will be before the bridge over the River Gadder, and immediately adjacent to the Anglian Water works. There may be signs warning of a bull in the field, so take care. (Alternatively return to the crossroads and turn left to walk into Oxborough by road.) Cross a stile and walk straight across the meadow ahead, aiming for a prominent hedgerow, until you reach another stile in the far corner of the field. Keep straight ahead with the hedgerow on your left and stay on the path, crossing over a track, until you reach a third stile. Cross the stile and walk between the houses to return to the village green.

WHERE TO EAT AND DRINK The Bedingfeld Arms is a lovely country pub overlooking the village green and the half-ruined Church of St John the Evangelist. It serves home-cooked food and has a large garden. There is a licensed restaurant inside Oxburgh Hall, open at variable times between March and November.

WHAT TO SEE One of Oxburgh Hall's best features is its tremendous, late 15th-century gatehouse, perhaps the best of its kind. It was so impressive that in 1487 Sir Edmund Bedingfeld was able to entertain Henry VII and his wife Elizabeth inside it. Don't miss the King's Room on the first floor of the gatehouse.

WHILE YOU'RE THERE Close by is Cockley Cley, which boasts a reconstructed Iceni village on the site of an original encampment. You can see houses, towers, defences and a drawbridge.

A Stroll Around King's Lynn

DISTANCE 4 miles (6.4km)   MINIMUM TIME 2hrs

ASCENT/GRADIENT Negligible ▲▲▲   LEVEL OF DIFFICULTY ✚✚

PATHS Pavements, cobbled streets, grassy river path and steps to ferry

LANDSCAPE Town buildings and open riverside

SUGGESTED MAP AA Leisure Map 6 North West Norfolk

START/FINISH Grid reference: TF620199

DOG FRIENDLINESS Lead required on town streets

PARKING Blackfriar Street car park or St James multi-storey

PUBLIC TOILETS At car park and various locations in town

NOTES Ferry operates 7am–6pm year-round, but not on Sundays or
Bank Holidays

King's Lynn was originally just called Lynn, and was an unassuming little place. But in the early Middle Ages, things began to take off. Lynn was strategically placed on one of the most important waterways in medieval England and soon a huge amount of trade was passing through. The town exported corn from Lincolnshire, lead from Derbyshire, salt from Norfolk and Lincolnshire and, most importantly, wool from the East Midlands. It imported dried cod from Iceland and timber, pitch and resin from the Baltic, as well as Flemish and Italian cloths.

With all these revenues, Lynn became a wealthy place, and Herbert de Losinga, the first Bishop of Norwich, decided he wanted it for himself. It became known as Bishop's Lynn, and so remained until the 1530s, when Henry VIII squashed its ecclesiastical association and named it King's Lynn, after himself. The change in name meant little to Lynn's merchants, who remained prosperous and continued to build their grand houses and churches, many of which can still be seen today.

A CHEQUERED HISTORY

King's Lynn is an architectural dream, with almost every period represented, ranging from St Nicholas's Chapel, built between 1145 and 1420, to picturesque Burkitt Court Almshouses, built in 1909 in memory of a Lynn corn merchant. One of the most visible landmarks is the 14th-century Greyfriars Tower, once part of a Franciscan Friary. The beautifully proportioned Custom House, now a tourist information centre, was built in 1683 as a merchants' exchange. St George's Guildhall is the largest surviving guildhall in England. It was built around 1410, and has been used as a warehouse, a store for guns during the Civil War and a court house. It is now the King's Lynn Artscentre.

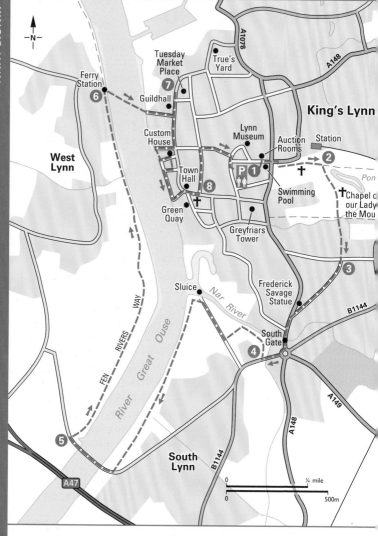

1 From the car park, head for King's Lynn Auction Rooms, pass the fitness centre and swimming pool and cross the road to the park. Take the path towards the Church of St John the Evangelist.

2 Turn right by the pond. On a little knoll to your left is the redbrick Chapel of Our Lady of the Mount, built in 1485 for pilgrims travelling to Walsingham. When you reach the ruinous walls of the

town's defences, continue on the path straight ahead with the football ground to your left.

3 Keep straight ahead into Guanock Terrace, passing The Beeches guest house and Lord Napier pub to the statue of Mayor Frederick Savage. Bear left at London Road towards the 15th-century South Gate, then cross the road. Walk past the Gate and turn right at the roundabout. Cross a bridge over the river and take the

Nar Valley Way, signposted to the right immediately after the bridge.

④ This is the final stretch of the Way, which follows the river to the Nar Outfall Sluice, where it meets the Great Ouse. Keep to the bottom of the bank until about 150yds (137m) after a sharp left bend. Scramble up the bank and walk away from the river, beside a concrete wall, until a handgate leads onto a road. Turn right along the road to the sluice and then take the path to the left along the east river bank. After 0.75 miles (1.2km), turn right over the bridge.

⑤ Turn right on the far side of the bridge onto the Fen Rivers Way. Follow this path for just over a mile (1.6km), with views across the river to King's Lynn. Initially, the path is grassy, but then becomes a raised walkway leading to the ferry station.

⑥ Take the ferry (runs every 20 minutes) back to King's Lynn. Walk up Ferry Lane as far as King Street. Turn left to see the Tuesday Market

Place with its 750-seat Corn Exchange concert hall.

⑦ Retrace your steps past Ferry Lane and continue to Purfleet Quay, which houses the Custom House and a statue of explorer George Vancouver, Lynn's most famous son. At the end of the quay, cross the bridge and walk across the square. Take a narrow lane opposite to reach cobbled King's Staithe Lane. Turn right to return to the river bank, then head left to Thoresby College, built in 1500 for 13 chantry priests. Turn left to walk along College Lane to reach the Saturday Market Place. Bear right and then left, passing the attractive chequered Town Hall and Old Gaol House, with St Margaret's Church dominating the square.

⑧ Turn left onto the pedestrian High Street for a flavour of the modern town. At the crossroads, turn right along New Conduit Street, then right again on Tower Street. Take the alley to the left opposite the Majestic Cinema to return to the car park.

WHERE TO EAT AND DRINK True's Yard and the Green Quay have friendly cafes, and there are plenty of cafes and restaurants in the pedestrian section of town. The Tudor Rose hotel dates from the 15th century and claims to be the most haunted place in the town.

WHAT TO SEE The walk passes the fascinating Tales of the Old Gaol House. This museum explores the darker side of the town, looking at smuggling, witches and crime.

WHILE YOU'RE THERE There are a number of attractions off the walk. These include True's Yard, which explores the harsh realities of life as a fisherman in old King's Lynn. The Green Quay has an interactive discovery centre dedicated to the Wash. The Lynn Museum concentrates on local history. If you have time for a longer excursion, you can take the Peter Scott Walk, north along the Great Ouse from West Lynn.

Walpoles in the Marshes

DISTANCE 7.25 miles (11.7km)	MINIMUM TIME 3hrs

ASCENT/GRADIENT Negligible ▲▲▲   LEVEL OF DIFFICULTY ✚✚✚

PATHS Footpaths in fields and housing estates, country lanes

LANDSCAPE Pancake-flat fenland and prairie-style fields

SUGGESTED MAP OS Explorer 236 King's Lynn, Downham Market & Swaffham

START/FINISH Grid reference: TF520199

DOG FRIENDLINESS Dogs can run free

PARKING Near war memorial, Walpole Cross Keys

PUBLIC TOILETS None on route

In October 1216, things were not looking good for King John of England. The previous year he had been forced to sign Magna Carta, which saw him abrogate much of his regal power to the barons, and 11 months later Prince Louis of France invaded the country, intending to seize the English crown for himself. King Alexander of Scotland had reached Cambridge and had to be ousted, and John was losing supporters by the fistful. To top it all, he was ill, probably with dysentery – unpleasant at any time, but especially so when travelling fast along a medieval road.

KING JOHN'S LOST TREASURE

On 11 October, John started to move from his Norfolk base into Lincolnshire. Because time was of the essence, with hostile forces all around, he was obliged to take the shortest and quickest route. This happened to be across the Wellstream Estuary in Walpole St Andrew. Impatient to be on his way, John didn't wait for the tide to recede and the result was devastating. The heavy baggage wagons became bogged down in the mud and many of the servants driving them drowned. He also lost some of his chapel goods.

Did John lose the crown jewels in the Wash as the monk chroniclers at St Albans later claimed? Did the tide come racing in, to suck the King's entire baggage train, all his money and most of his army into quicksands and whirlpools? Probably not, although the legend persists and the Walpoles have seen countless treasure hunters searching for the fabled lost wealth. Within a few days John was dead. His servants stole his personal goods, the Abbot of Croxton laid claim to his intestines for burial in his abbey, and his nine-year-old son was crowned Henry III.

CATHEDRAL OF THE FENS

The Walpoles offer a good deal more than legends, however. There are four of them – St Andrew, St Peter, Cross Keys and Highway. The church at Walpole St Peter is so magnificent that it is known as the 'Cathedral of the Fens'. It was originally built in Saxon times, but was swept away by floods in 1337, so much of what you see today dates from the mid-14th to 15th centuries. Little Walpole Highway's church was built in 1844 as a chapel of ease for people who found Walpole St Peter's too far to travel.

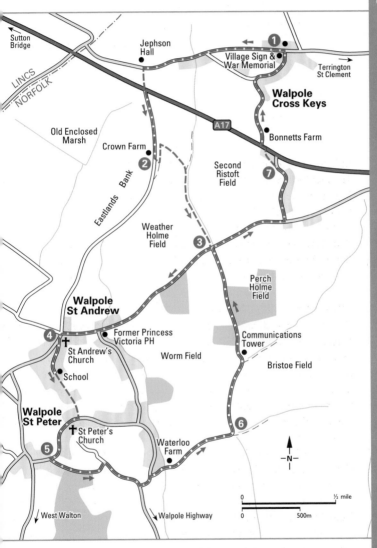

❶ With the village sign behind you, turn left along Sutton Road, using the pavement on the right-hand side. After about 0.75 miles (1.2km), just before Jephson Hall, you will see a track named Eastlands Bank on your left. Follow it, cross the A17 with care, and head down the lane opposite, signed 'No access to the Walpoles'. This lane follows the line of ancient sea defences; continue along it for about 500yds (457m), opposite Crown Farm.

2 Take the descending track to the left and then dogleg back northwards below the bank for about 87yds (80m), until you can turn right over a culvert. Follow the path beside a ditch along the edge of two fields before emerging onto a grassy track, where you turn right. Eventually you pass some buildings to arrive at a crossroads.

3 Turn right and walk down the lane into the village of Walpole St Andrew. Continue until you reach the old Princess Victoria pub, dating from 1651 and now a private house. Keep straight ahead at the junction along Wisbech Road until you see St Andrew's Church to your left.

4 Bear left at the crossroads at St Andrew's Church. Take the first turn on your left and walk down this road towards the primary school. Take the footpath that runs down the side of the school and through a housing estate, to emerge near the church in Walpole St Peter. Turn right, using the pavement on the right as the road winds around to another junction.

5 Turn sharp left, signposted towards Walpole Highway, and stay on this road as it winds through the village. Turn left at Chalk Road. After the road bends, turn right into Bustards Lane and continue until you reach a bend with a farm track straight ahead.

6 Keep to the road as it bends left and walk until you see a communications tower on your right. Keep left again and after 0.5 miles (800m) you will reach the junction you made earlier at Point **3**. Go right, with greenhouses to your left, until you reach another junction. Turn left, and follow the lane until you see a tall fence and a hedge of Leylandii trees.

7 Bear left beside a reconstruction of the former Walpole railway station platform, passing The Old Railway Inn, now a house, to reach the A17. Follow the pavement to the left, then cross over at the end of the railings, using the central island. On the other side, walk to the left of the piled pallets and up the lane past scattered houses and a fruit farm. At the T-junction turn right along Station Road and continue back to the start of the walk.

WHERE TO EAT AND DRINK There are no refreshments along the route of the walk, but the nearby village of Terrington St Clement has a shop, bakery, fish and chips and a pizza restaurant. There are also two pubs, both of which serve food.

WHAT TO SEE Since Walpole St Peter has one of the most famous churches in East Anglia, it's worth looking around inside it. The wonderful south porch, at 1450 the latest addition to the building, is heavy with carved roof bosses. On the left, just through the doors, stands a strange sentry-box, known as a hudd, that was used to protect the minister from harsh fenland weather when conducting burials. And don't miss the Bolt Hole, a mysterious vaulted tunnel that runs under the west end of the church.

WHILE YOU'RE THERE Other marshland villages with mighty 'cathedrals' are West Walton, Wiggenhall St Mary, Terrington St Clement, Walsoken and Tilney All Saints. The Fenland Aviation Museum is at West Walton, southwest of Walpole St Peter.

Exploring Denver Sluice at Downham Market

DISTANCE 5.75 miles (9.2km)	MINIMUM TIME 2hrs 30min

ASCENT/GRADIENT 98ft (30m) ▲▲▲   LEVEL OF DIFFICULTY ✚✚✚

PATHS Riverside footpaths and country lanes, town streets

LANDSCAPE Flat fenland, river and drainage channels, arable farmland

SUGGESTED MAP OS Explorer 236 King's Lynn, Downham Market & Swaffham

START/FINISH Grid reference: TF611033

DOG FRIENDLINESS Keep dogs under control along river bank (livestock)

PARKING Town Council car park (free) in Paradise Road

PUBLIC TOILETS Opposite Town Hall in Market Square

One of the Downham Market area's most famous sons was George William Manby, born at Denver Hall. In February 1807, Manby was in Great Yarmouth when HMS *Snipe* was wrecked on a nearby sandbar. All attempts to reach it failed and, despite heroic efforts by local people, all hands were drowned. This traumatic experience affected Manby deeply, and he decided to find a way to secure a stricken ship to the shore.

Manby devised a manner in which a line could be connected to the shot fired from a mortar on shore to the ship. Then, to use that line to get stranded seamen ashore, he produced a small boat with a number of casks fixed as buoyancy chambers, developing the principle still used as a safety measure in small boats today. His apparatus was so successful that Parliament awarded him £2,000. Manby turned to a career as an inventor, including making harpoons and harpoon guns for the whaling industry.

DEFENDING THE LAND

Denver is famous for its sluices. The first was built by Cornelius Vermuyden to limit the tidal flow up the Great Ouse. The Duke of Bedford, who funded the project, was delighted to see his lands become viable for farming, but not everyone shared his sentiments. The Fen Tigers were a group who did not want to see their way of life changed by drainage. They blew up the sluice to make their point. Sailors and traders also resented the sluice, because it blocked the direct route to Cambridge and forced them to take their coal via Earith. The sluice was destroyed again in 1713, this time by the sea, and was rebuilt several times before Sir John Rennie designed the one which still exists today. It was remodelled and new steel gates added, most recently in 1983. The Denver Sluice (1959) stands on a newer waterway, called the Relief Channel.

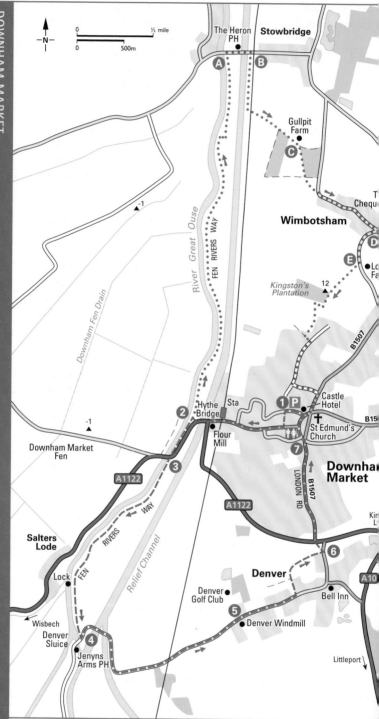

1 Leave the car park and turn right. When you reach Morrisons on your left, cut through its car park to a road running parallel to Paradise Road, and turn right. The road winds downhill, passing the White Hart pub, to a level crossing and the station. Continue past Heygates flour mill on your left, and cross Hythe Bridge over the Great Ouse Relief Channel. On the far side of the bridge cross a stile on your right. Walk along a track to a junction of paths by the river bank.

2 Take the left-hand fork, and cross a second stile to reach the Fen Rivers Way along the east bank of the Great Ouse. The banks have been raised to prevent flooding. After about 0.25 miles (400m) you reach a bridge.

3 Cross carefully over the busy A1122 and continue through a pair of gates to return to the river bank. The path continues until you reach the lock at Salters Lode. Proceed until the Denver Sluice comes into sight.

4 After exploring the sluice, turn left along the lane and cross the bridge over the Relief Channel. Keep to the lane as it winds through farmland and across a level crossing. After passing a huge field on your right, look for the white tower of Denver Windmill up ahead.

5 Pass the mill and continue along the lane for 0.5 miles (800m), then turn left up Sandy Lane. The lane becomes a track, which you follow until it ends at the junction with the B1507.

6 Turn left along the course of the old road, to reach the A1122. Cross this road carefully to reach London Road. Use the pavement on the left-hand side, passing the police station on your right. Eventually you reach a mini-roundabout with a Tesco supermarket on the left.

7 Keep straight ahead, then fork left past the war memorial and aim for the clock tower, walking along the High Street and through the market square to the Castle Hotel. Turn left at the hotel and walk down Paradise Road a few paces until you reach the car park.

WHERE TO EAT AND DRINK The Castle Hotel and Crown Hotel are 17th-century coaching inns near the start of the walk which both serve bar meals and real ales. At Denver Sluice, the Jenyns Arms is on the banks of the river, while the Bell Inn is in Denver itself. The Golf Club, set back from the road opposite the windmill, has a coffee shop which is open to the public and serves hot meals.

WHAT TO SEE Denver Windmill (1835) used the wind to grind corn for more than 100 years until it was hit by lightning in 1941. It was restored by the Norfolk Windmills Trust, but is closed again at the time of checking (February 2013) after damage to the sails.

WHILE YOU'RE THERE St Edmund's Church, which dominates the town, was severely restored by the Victorians, but retains many features dating from the 13th century on. See how many angels you can count – in the roof, the medieval stained glass of the tower windows, and the delicate roundels near the chancel arch.

Downham Market to Stowbridge

DISTANCE 6.5 miles (10.4km)   MINIMUM TIME 2hrs 45min

ASCENT/GRADIENT 98ft (30m) ▲▲▲   LEVEL OF DIFFICULTY ✦✦✦

SEE MAP AND INFORMATION PANEL FOR WALK 48

The narrow stretch of land that lies between the River Great Ouse and the Relief Channel is known as the Hythe, and it is along this that you spend the first part of the walk. The prosaically named Relief Channel was built to take the strain of water from the rivers Lark, Little Ouse and Wissey from the Great Ouse, taking its load on a more direct route to the sea.

The footpath along the east bank of the Great Ouse is part of the Fen Rivers Way, a long distance trail that follows public footpaths, historical drovers' routes and quiet lanes through fenland countryside.

Begin at Point ❷, and take the right-hand fork to walk north along the Fen Rivers Way. This is along the levied banks of the River Great Ouse, giving superb views across the Fens. After about 2.5 miles (4km) of peaceful walking you reach a set of gates, Point ❹. Go through the gates and turn right, passing The Heron pub and crossing the bridge over the Relief Channel. Immediately after the bridge, and before the level crossing, look for a waymark on the right to lead you down the east bank of the Relief Channel.

Pass through a gate, Point ❺, and walk for about 650yds (594m) until the path turns left across the railway line and becomes a track. Stay on this track for around 700yds (640m). When you see Gullpit Farm cottage on your left, Point ❻, look for a footpath to the right. The path skirts the edge of a wood before turning left then right across a wide track, crossing a field diagonally and crossing a footbridge to emerge on a minor road. Turn right and follow the road round to the left to enter the village of Wimbotsham.

Turn right on the green (Point ❼) by the village sign and walk until you reach Lower Farm. Opposite the farm, on your right, is a waymarked footpath, Point ❽. Take this and follow the wide track towards Kingston's Plantation. At the end of the Plantation keep to the right of the field boundary, following a path which crosses a footbridge and runs behind a housing estate to arrive on Wimbotsham Road. Turn right and stay on this road as it bends left to become Clackclose Road and climbs gently to the B1507. Turn right, and keep right at the traffic lights opposite St Edmund's Church, then right again at the Castle Hotel to the car park.

Welney's Wetlands

DISTANCE 4 miles (6.4km)   MINIMUM TIME 1hr 30min

ASCENT/GRADIENT Negligible ▲▲▲   LEVEL OF DIFFICULTY ✦✦✦

PATHS Boardwalks and grass paths with benches

LANDSCAPE Reedy wetlands, lagoons and fen

SUGGESTED MAP OS Explorer 228 March & Ely

START/FINISH Grid reference: TL546944

DOG FRIENDLINESS Dogs not permitted

PARKING WWT Welney car park, signposted off A1101

PUBLIC TOILETS At visitor centre

NOTES The path is closed during the nesting season, and because of winter
flooding it is usually only open between June and September. Contact Welney
Wetland Centre (01353 860711; www.wwt.org.uk) to check route is open. Pay
at visitor centre to enter the reserve

The Wildfowl and Wetlands Trust (WWT) reserve at Welney Washes is
tucked away in the southwest corner of Norfolk, on the border with
Cambridgeshire. It covers 850 acres (344ha) of freshwater grazing
marshland that floods regularly – the largest such area remaining in
Britain. This unique habitat was formed when two massive drainage
channels were created, leaving a strip of land between them that is
about 0.5 miles (800m) wide. This area is known as the Ouse Washes,
and it acts as a reservoir to hold excess water when the main drainage
system is unable to cope.

DRAINING THE FENS

Several attempts were made to drain the Fens – by the Romans and
by medieval engineers – but it was not until the 17th century that
this wilderness of sedge, reed and bog was finally vanquished. The
wealthy Duke of Bedford wanted to do more with the fenland than
graze sheep in the summer and watch it flood all winter. He employed
Dutch engineer Cornelius Vermuyden to design a new river system that
would allow flood water to be channelled more directly out to sea.
The cut between Earith in Cambridgeshire and Denver in Norfolk was
named the Old Bedford River and was completed in 1637. Although
it vastly improved the Duke's summer grazing grounds, his land still
flooded in winter. A second cut was made, running parallel to the first,
and called the New Bedford River. The banks on both rivers were raised,
so that the area between them could take surplus water during times of
flood – creating the Ouse Washes.

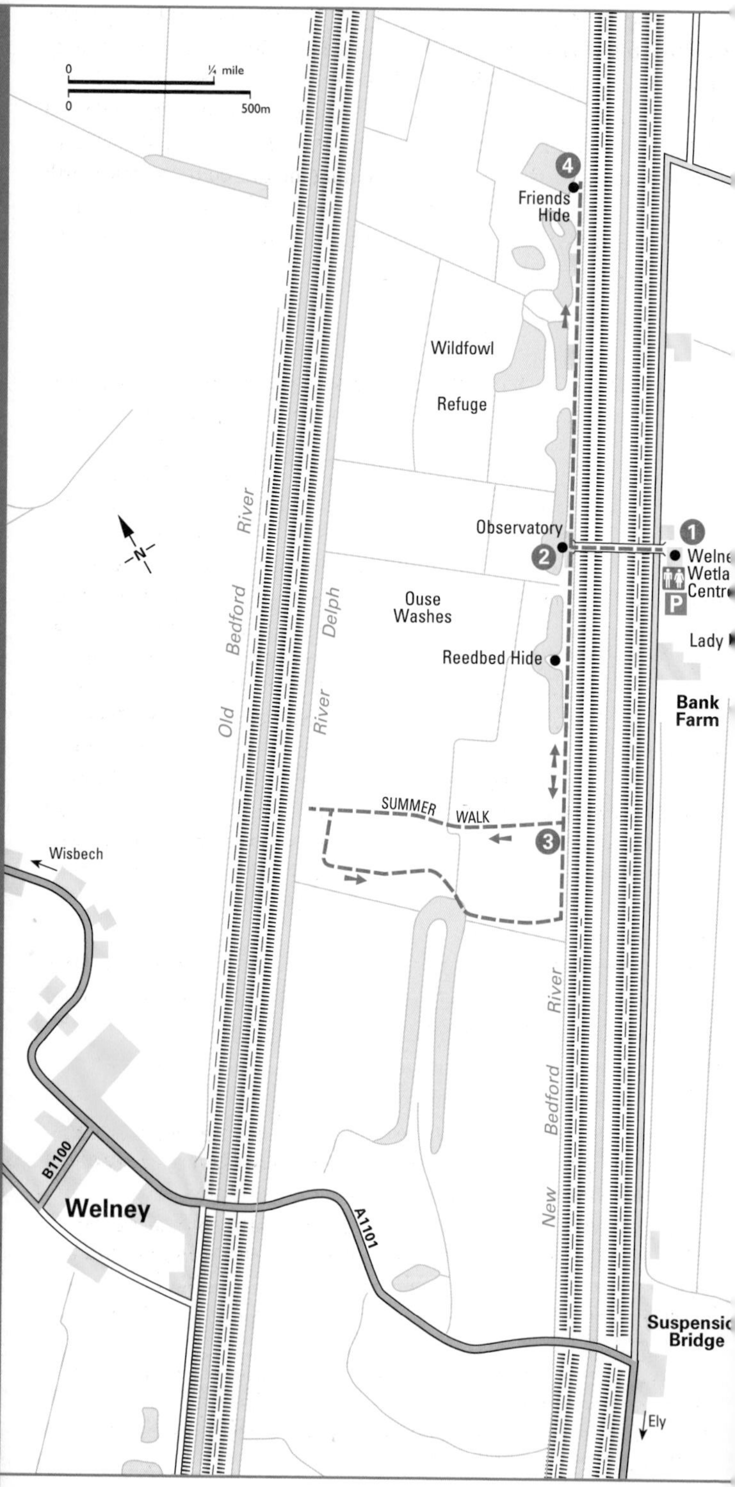

¼ mile
0
0   500m

④
Friends
Hide

Wildfowl

Refuge

Old Bedford River

River Delph

Observatory
②

Ouse
Washes

Reedbed Hide

SUMMER   WALK
③

Wisbech

① Welne
● Wetla
Centre
P
Lady

Bank
Farm

New Bedford River

B1100

Welney

A1101

Suspensic
Bridge

Ely

-N-

A visit to Welney is magical at any time of year (although this walking route is only accessible in summer time). The eco-friendly Wetland Centre, built from local timber and opened in 2006, has interesting exhibitions and operates using solar power, undersoil heating and toilets flushed with rainwater. Best of all, the reserve provides some of the finest birdwatching in the country. It's worth visiting in November, when thousands of Bewick's swans arrive from Russia and whooper swans come from Iceland to overwinter on the fens, before returning in spring.

1 After buying your ticket, climb the stairs or take the lift from the visitor centre to gain access to the reserve. Walk across the footbridge then follow the ramp down to the left to enter the observatory.

2 Continue down another ramp and turn right at the bottom, following signs to the Summer Walk. The first section of the walk is known as the Screen Bank Walk. Soon signs will direct you to the right to the Reedbed Hide and dragonfly ponds. Continue along the Screen Bank Walk until you see a sign to your right for the Summer Walk.

3 The Summer Walk is the only route anywhere with public access to the Ouse Washes. If it is open, turn right to walk beneath the telegraph poles. The route itself varies from year to year, but follow the waymarks and information panels for an easy self-guided trail through the wild flowers and grassland. The picnic benches beside the pond are a good place to observe dragonflies. After completing the Summer Walk, return to the Screen Bank Walk, turn left and retrace your steps to the observatory and footbridge. At the footbridge, continue straight ahead, along the northern part of the Screen Bank Walk. Eventually you reach Nelson-Lyle Hide, Lyle Hide, Allport Hide and Friends Hide, all on your left. This part of the walk is linear, but you will see so many different birds that it won't feel like it.

4 At Friends Hide, retrace your steps back to the footbridge, cross it, and return to the car park.

WHERE TO EAT AND DRINK The Wigeon Café in the visitor centre serves hot meals, sandwiches, cakes and drinks, and has a pleasant terrace overlooking the 200 acres (81ha) of the created wetland, Lady Fen.

WHAT TO SEE Don't miss a spell in the WWT's observatory looking over the main lagoon. Twenty wildfowl species have been recorded here, but most impressive are the sheer numbers of birds that arrive in winter. Counts have included 3,000 Bewick's swans, 1,000 whooper swans and an impressive 30,000 wigeon.

WHILE YOU'RE THERE Visit the Fenland Worlds exhibition in the visitor centre, which explores the history and ecology of the Fens. There are displays on fenland traditions, including wildfowling and ice skating, and the floods which regularly devastate the area.

Titles in the Series